M000201795

CUSTOMER SUCCESS MINDSET

Building customer-centricity
into the DNA of your
growth strategy

JYO SHUKLA

Customer Success Mindset

© 2022 Jyotsana Shukla, Sydney, Australia

Publication date April 2022

The moral right of the author has been asserted. All rights reserved. Without limiting the rights under copyright reserved above, no part of this publication may be reproduced, distributed, or transmitted in any form or by any means, stored in or introduced to a retrieval system or transmitted in any form of by any means (electronic, mechanical, photocopying, recording or otherwise), without the prior consent of the author and the publisher of the book.

Cover design by The Copy Collective Pty Ltd TA Red Raven Books
Typeset in Roboto
Typeset & Layout © The Copy Collective Pty Ltd TA Red Raven Books
Level 2, 194 Varsity Pde, Varsity Lakes Qld 4277

Print on Demand, ePub

Shukla, Jyotsana, author.
    Customer Success Mindset, Jyotsana Shukla
    ISBN: 978-0-6453577-0-7 (paperback)
            978-0-6453577-2-1 (casebound)
            978-0-6453577-1-4 (epdf)
    Subjects: Business, Non Fiction
    Customer Success – Australia
    Leadership - Australia

A catalogue record for this work is available on request from the National Library of Australia.

NATIONAL
LIBRARY OF AUSTRALIA

Visit www.customersuccessmindset.com to access, download and share all your favourite quotes and graphics from this book.

Scan the QR Code below to visit the website

Dedicated to my family.
I am nothing without you all!

Advance Praise for *Customer Success Mindset*

In her book, Jyo lays out what I believe is one of the clearest blueprints on how to design, execute, and benefit from a company-wide mindset of customer-led growth. Customer Success Mindset is a must-read for customer success leaders and other executives who aspire to deliver sustainable growth to their organizations.
- Alex Farmer, VP of Customer Success, Cognite and Founder of Customer Excellence - The Customer Success Awards

This book captures the essence of customer-centricity, defining a clear path for businesses to bring continual value to customers throughout their customer success journey.
- Dickey Singh, Founder and CEO, cast.app

"This is like a 5-star cookbook for Customer Success - it's filled with recipes and the ingredients you need to create a value-filled journey for your customers."
- Laura E. Beavin Yates, SVP of Customer Success, Immersion Neuroscience

"Jyo is pushing customer success thinking forward by providing a practical guide for companies to use a customer success mindset as a growth strategy. A must-read for folks - regardless if you are in customer success or not - who want to supercharge their growth strategies!"
- Jennifer Chiang, Author of *The Startup's Guide to Customer Success*, Top 50 CS Woman Leader and Head of Customer Success at Seso

This is a must-read for anyone looking for a step by step guide to creating a truly customer-centric culture. I've been lucky to watch Jyo translate her passion, skills and mindset into our daily activities across our team and this book captures the spirit in which she does it!
- James Ellender, CEO, ActiveXchange

"Customer Success Mindset dives into some important questions companies need to answer. Why is getting your customers to rave about your products not enough? Why are some companies struggling with pricing conversations even as they race to the bottom?
Jyo's language is crisp and clear with specific examples and tools. Highly recommended"
- Jesus Jimenez Berrocal, Director, Customer Success, Cisco APJC

"It's clear reading Jyo's book that she embraces a Customer Success Mindset and she does an awesome job sharing her knowledge with the community. It is a wonderful guide of information for everyone from the entry-level CSM to the experienced Chief Customer Officer. I highly recommend adding Customer Success Mindset to your library!"

- Brian Nicholls, Vice President of Customer Success, UserIQ

"In Customer Success, as in life, the mindset plays a big role in how humans evolve. The Customer Success Mindset helps businesses tap into both the philosophy of Customer Success and the execution of that philosophy. Jyo's work hits the right balance of education and actionable advice to help any company that runs on a subscription model to achieve success – both for itself and its customers."

- Anita Toth, Churn and VOC Consultant

"Jyo provides a thoughtful, modern, and refreshing take on maximizing the value provided from Customer Success. I'd recommend Customer Success Mindset to any leaders working to build and improve Customer Success teams and to any individuals serious about building a long term career in this space."

- Pat Puentes, Director Global Customer Success, BitSight

"What Jyo has achieved is an easy to follow guide, firstly allowing anyone to easily understand whether they are truly customer-centric, and secondly laying out clear steps on what you need to take to become one. To only have the CS team at your business read this book would ignore Jyo's key message that customer-centricity must be embraced by the whole organization if you want to achieve growth, so get everyone in your org a copy!"

- Alix Simpson,
Vice President of Customer Success, Partnerize

CONTENTS

ACKNOWLEDGEMENTS

Customer Success Mindset may have my name on the front page, but it really is the collective work of so many people whose inputs, thoughts, and constructive criticism have made it a reality.

This book is a testament to how collaborative the global customer success community is.

This community really "walks the talk" in displaying the spirit of help, growth and sharing knowledge with their peers as much as they do in their professional lives with customers. I am amazed at all the help that came back my way to refine my ideas for the book; all I did was ask.

First of all, I want to thank Rav Dhaliwal of Crane Venture Partners for penning down the foreword. I have learnt so much from all of Rav's contributions to the world of customer success based on his experience leading customer success at Slack, Yammer, and Zendesk. Having him write the foreword is nothing short of an honour.

Aden Forrest, your invaluable inputs and feedback have helped shape my overall thinking and approach toward the book. I don't think any amount of thanks is enough for the advice, time and encouragement you have offered. Dickey Singh, your work is inspiring the future of digital customer success; thank you for taking the time to thoroughly read my draft and offer your invaluable suggestions.

Jesus Jimenez, Pat Puentes, and James Ellender, working with each one of you has been full of so many learnings, and I cannot begin to describe how much your time in reading my draft means to me. You all are my stars.

A huge thank you to Anita Toth and Laura E. Beavin-Yates, who have not only contributed to the book but have also given so many tips and recommendations that aided my thought process. Jennifer Chiang, your thoughts and positivity around the writing process really supercharged me and prepared me to give it my best shot.

Ed Powers, I don't think the chapter on data would be the same without your input. Maranda Dzienoski, your work as a CCO is beyond inspirational, thank you for all your positivity and your time. Heidi Rhodes, I've looked up to your work since my customer success days at Cisco; thank you for your invaluable time and contribution.

Prakhar Rawat, who has not only lent his deep technology expertise and understanding of Software-as-a-Service, but also supported me through sleepless nights and happy days as my husband.

Maureen Shelley and Kim Peñaflorida of Red Raven Publishing for a seamless publishing process and for answering my questions patiently all along.

My family has an invaluable contribution to this book. My Mum and Dad, who instilled the love of books in me at a very young age. My son Ryan, who has taught me the value of patience and empathy at the tender age of 3, and my husband Prakhar (I love him too much, so I'll thank him twice!).

To everyone I might have missed in here, please accept my sincerest apologies and know that I am the clumsiest person on the face of the earth, but that doesn't speak to the value of your contribution to this book or my life.

Jyo

FOREWORD

Software companies have become such a ubiquitous part of modern life, that a quick internet search reveals a plethora of articles, blog posts and books dedicated to the best ways to build, scale and run one.

Whilst incredibly valuable, this material rarely covers what, in my view, is one of the *most* critical aspects of running a successful software company - its "mindset".

A company's "mindset" can be described as the set of beliefs it holds that shape not only how it makes sense of the world, but that greatly influence how it thinks, behaves and acts in any given situation.

Stanford psychologist Carol Dweck states that beliefs play a pivotal role in what individuals want and whether they achieve it.

This is equally true for companies in my experience, with some believing that their behaviour and actions should primarily be in service of their investors and shareholders, whilst others believing that the impact on their employees and society at large should determine their priorities and actions.

Regardless of the specific beliefs any one particular company may hold, according to Dweck, all beliefs fall into two basic mindsets: *fixed* and *growth*.

With a fixed mindset, an individual or company believes that their abilities cannot be changed and that talent and intelligence alone (not effort), are what leads to success.

On the other side, Dweck posits that with a growth mindset, an individual or company believes that its talents and abilities can be developed over time through continual sustained effort, and that success can always be achieved if they persistently work on it.

All of which leads me neatly to this book and why, when asked, I was delighted to contribute this foreword.

What Jyo has fashioned here is a deeply personal and practical reflection on just what it takes to develop that *growth* mindset and more importantly she shows from her own experience that the actual key to success for companies is a belief that it is the *customer* that needs to be at the centre of how they view the world and operate.

Whilst there are many companies that claim that *"customers are at the heart of what we do"*, too often just a little scratching beneath the surface reveals this to be (sadly) a platitude.

In the pages that follow, Jyo casts an uncynical eye on why this might be the case and what practical steps and actions she's learned that companies can take to inculcate a *"Customer Success Mindset"* that not only benefits them, but all their internal and external stakeholders.

Rav Dhaliwal

INTRODUCTION

Remember the times when entertainment on the internet was not such a huge thing as it is today, and new song videos and movie trailers were launched on television? (shoutout to my readers who grew up in the mid-2000s). The media created a big hype around what time and date a new song or movie preview was going to be released on entertainment channels. Teenagers would stay glued to their television sets close to the time of the launch, eagerly waiting to get the first glimpse of all the latest songs and movie previews.

I remember getting calls on my landline from my friends, squealing with excitement at the other end of the line. *"Have you watched it yet? Go do it now, you'll love that song"*. They made the recommendation so strongly as if their life depended on it. What did they get in return? Nothing, except for the sheer joy of seeing their friends liking what they liked and earning their trust and companionship. Everyone enjoys being the cool kid; plus you'd get a series of recommendations of good television content from your friends in return (I called it a win-win at that point in my life).

The human desire to be social and to be appreciated by one's peers in their professional and personal lives forms the basis of networking. In fact, the business world, in particular, relies on the power of networking and shared knowledge. Whether it's receiving feedback on your ideas or sharing perspectives, people rely on their network to expand their knowledge and to stay abreast with the latest innovations that make their lives easier and better.

And the givers' gain in sharing recommendations about the latest best things they have tried is immense. The mutual assistance that comes from selflessly sharing recommendations and helping others brings back a whole world of opportunities. People use the power of their recommendations and perspectives to maintain and enhance their reputations. The latest advancements in technology or that cool new software that saves you heaps of time is always doing the rounds in business conversations in boardrooms, meetings, conferences and even over coffee and food. But here's the thing, with their personal reputation at stake, people only recommend solutions that they have tried and tested themselves and can attest to the value of. They have to believe in it to talk about it with their peers in the industry and business community.

The *Customer Success Mindset* taps into this very concept of human psychology. By winning the hearts and minds of people who use your product or service, and showcasing the change and value it brings into their professional lives and their way of working, you create raving fans that can't wait to tell their network about how your business made their work-life better. Companies that recognize this simple facet of human psychology will understand the importance of turning as many customers as they can into loyal advocates.

If the thought of turning a majority of your customers into brand advocates sounds wishful to you in the ever so practical world of business, think again. The fact is that in the current world, people get to experience the bliss of their customers doing the selling for them only so rarely that they think that it is not worth the effort, time and investment that goes into being a customer-centric organization.

The challenge is not getting a small percentage of your customers to be raving fans of your business; the *real* challenge is in scaling and operationalizing this mindset to build a partnership of advocacy and trust with the majority of your customers. And when you understand the opportunity and the personal and business growth that comes with having such a mindset, you will realize that the investment in being consciously and constantly customer-centric is more than worth it.

It is important to note that customer-centricity is different from customer-friendliness, customer-focus and customer service. These could all be thought of as *components* of customer-centricity. What customer-centricity really is about, is aligning the strategy for your long-term profitability to the needs and outcomes of your most valuable customers, and in doing that you positively impact your entire customer base, your brand value and your bottom line.

The path from customer-centricity to business growth can be simply laid out as follows:

- **Develop** a Customer Success Mindset
- **Operationalize** Customer-Centricity
- **Strategize** your Customer-Led Growth
- **Experience** Growth and Profitability for your business

And there you have it, a healthy **DOSE** of a sustainable growth model for your business (advance notice to my dear readers, you are only beginning to see my love for acronyms here!)

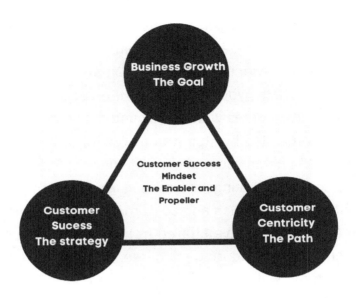

So, the big question is, where do you begin? As a business, how do you fuel your expansion using the power of customer-centricity? And how does this book fit into all of this?

Being truly customer-centric is more than just saying that you are, and is also not an easy journey to take. This book will not paint a picture of perfection to say customer-centricity is the silver bullet that skyrockets your revenue potential and fixes every single problem you have in your business. In fact, a huge part of understanding the concepts and methods outlined in this book is to "accept" that change is hard and to see the "opportunity" that comes from taking steps towards being more customer-centric than you are today.

What I aim to give you, is a starting point that helps you evaluate where you are in your journey towards customer-centricity, and what next steps you need to take. It helps you understand the opportunity for growth that comes with being customer-centric, and gives you a step by step framework that guides you along and helps you make simple tweaks to the way you do everyday things at work and in your interactions with your colleagues and customers. I firmly believe in the practices I've shared in this book and have seen them work during my career. Let's be real, not everything will work for everyone, and not everyone will be able to implement every single thing mentioned in the book. But like everything else we do, let us strive for a perfect world but live in a real one and make practical changes that work best for you as an individual, the team that you lead, your business and most importantly, your customers.

This book is for anyone who wants to drive greater value in their professional role by gaining an understanding of how customer-centricity and customer success are closely tied with business growth, and the role each individual can play (no matter what team they are part of), in fueling this growth. Whether you run or work for a large enterprise or a small to medium-sized business, your board and investors want to see an optimal internal rate of return for all projects that they allocate budgets for. Businesses of all sizes aim to grow exponentially while scaling their teams, processes and operations in the right way on a limited budget. If you were to find a way to enable your customers to promote the value of what you offer, and not only do the buying for themselves but also bring their friends, wouldn't you be unlocking a goldmine of growth? And all of this while streamlining your teams, breaking silos and improving operational efficiency. That's the long term effect of ingraining the *customer success mindset* into your teams, leadership and operations.

The steps outlined in the chapters that follow will help you get a jumpstart on the journey of understanding, building and scaling the *customer success mindset* across your business and into the DNA of how you operate. After that, you press the accelerator to keep going forward at your own pace. Will we be at a point where every company is 100% customer-centric? Now that is the wishful bit. That is like thinking everyone will be first in their class or that everyone will win the lotto. There will always be companies that do this better than you and others that don't do it so well. The key is to outline customer-centricity goals for the unique journey of your business.

I've divided the content of this book into three parts:

- **Part I : Understand (Chapters 1 to 3)**
  Chapters 1, 2, and 3 are all about understanding the customer success mindset. They help you understand what customer success and customer-led growth are all about, the anatomy of subscription-based relationships, and the importance of a company-wide customer success program.

- **Part II: Build, Measure and Execute (Chapters 4 to 8)**
  Part II talks about execution. We will look at practical steps that help you in building the customer success mindset into different phases of your customer's journey and incorporating it into the roles of different departments within your organization.

  We will then foray into the magical world of customer data, talk about identifying the right data points and using them to your advantage, the importance of customer feedback and building an effective voice of customer program, and educating your team on the value of each data point. And then, once we have the right data, how it can be used to fuel effective customer conversations in a high-touch program and build a personalized scale-touch model for connecting with all segments of your customers.

- **Part III: Grow (Chapters 9 and 10)**
  Part III outlines how you can reap the fruits of customer-centricity. We talk about the accountability and responsibility for ensuring smooth renewals, the future of customer success and how you can use your customer success and advocacy program to fuel the growth of your business.

The power is in your customers' hands, and you need to put them at the forefront of your strategy.

Ready?

Let's get started.

Part I: Understand

Chapter 1
CUSTOMER SUCCESS

Lessons from the Diary of a Shopaholic

I'm a 90's kid whose first love was books. My Dad introduced me to the magical world of Enid Blyton at the tender age of 4, and there was no looking back from there. I started to read everything I could get my hands on, from kids' fiction to encyclopaedias. Books were my happy place as a child, and reading still remains one of my favourite things to do when I'm trying to unwind.

But this book is not about my love for books. The fun fact in the above story is that as a kid, I purchased all my books from a single store, a quaint, old place owned by a kind, gentle woman named Miss B. I flat out refused to take my business elsewhere even though my Dad had to drive a fair bit to take me to Miss B's store every other weekend. I'd look forward to my visit and still have very vivid memories of the way the books were arranged on wooden, slightly dusty shelves that Miss B would often wipe down before handing me a title. She'd pick out books for me once I became a regular customer, based on titles I had bought before. I loved how she always greeted me with the kindest smile, gave me personal attention even when her store was jam-packed with other customers, and patiently answered all my silly questions: *Why did she think I would like a particular story? What was so good about it? What would I learn from it?* (Take it from me first-hand, I was one heck of an annoying kid!).

Over time, the range of reading media I used changed from paper books to electronic tablets and audiobook apps, and I experienced the joy of visiting some of the most beautiful bookstores across the globe. But to this day, I credit Miss B for nurturing my budding love of reading.

Miss B's store is more than just a childhood memory that will be forever etched in my mind; it was also my first exposure to the feeling of being valued as a customer. Good old Miss B's experience-centric ways of operating her small but hugely successful bookshop have more than a few lessons in store for us. Even though she may not have been a seller of enterprise products or services, Miss B sure had the mindset to treat her customers right and put their needs and emotions above everything else. From personalized attention to meaningful recommendations and group readings that attracted massive crowds of people, Miss B did all it takes to get to know a customer well, keep them happy, and create memorable experiences that would keep them coming back to her store. I might have realized it quite late in my life, but Miss B gave me my first lesson in customer success.

Growing up, I have become a person who, like most of us, loves to buy new things. Every shiny new item I see, be it the latest gadget or a cool new appliance, my mind creates a use case for it in my life. But I also very quickly lose interest in my once shiny-new belongings. And then those items become mere decorations or find their place inside cupboards that are rarely opened. I'm sure you have experienced something similar, and have a tiny (or huge!) stash of things that seemed to make so much sense when you bought them but don't anymore. And this tells us a very important thing about the way people consume goods and services: *It is quite easy to get people to feel they need something before they buy it, but keeping that interest alive and having them come back for more is an uphill task.*

The above page from the diary of a shopaholic can easily fit into the world of software products and services. We live in a world where digital transformation is a constant for businesses in every niche, but technology overload is also very real. Everyone is looking to get ahead in the game using the power of technology, but the plethora of choices makes it hard to not only choose the right fit product or service, but also to be successful with your choice in the long run.

A recent study conducted by PriceWaterhouseCoopers[1] reveals that organizations who were 'winning' in the marketplace had one thing in common: Digital Transformation. One of the key things these organizations acknowledged was that as much as technology is supporting their vision, it's also the ability to differentiate themselves when technology is used well that is important to them. Technology helps companies create better insights, introduce automation for key capabilities and enables them to scale efficiently, but the key is to ensure that it is adopted well and used right by all parts of the business, continually and effectively.

Many companies have the business equivalent of our cupboard of unused items, full of technical solutions which do not quite seem to have delivered the outcomes they promised. The challenge when you sell software as a service (or anything for that matter), is how to stay out of that cupboard. Because in the world of subscriptions, no business is going to continue paying for products and services that are not delivering the right outcomes for them in the short and long run.

In such a scenario, the role of technology solution providers goes beyond just selling products and services. What you sell is important, how you sell it

---

[1]   The Evolving Customer: Profile of a Winner, PwC, 2020

is also important; but what do you do to keep your customers engaged after that sale has happened, how you make sure they get optimal value out of your offering, what do you do to ensure it stays relevant and aligned to their short and long term goals and how it fits into their strategy in the future is the key to unlocking the mystery box labelled *"How to get your customers to stay engaged and be successful"*.

In the world of subscriptions, customer success is a proven strategy used by companies to help foster stronger relationships with customers, leading to increased retention, advocacy and growth for a business. Customer success is built around the foundations of proactively partnering with customers throughout their journey and helping them receive maximum value out of their purchase.

Customer Success has been around for decades in the world of software as a service (SaaS). However, its definition and expected outcomes have evolved over the years. What was initially thought of as a job role or function that was created to help prevent revenue churn was first turned into an expansion mechanism for upselling and cross-selling additional offerings and then further into a system to enhance customer advocacy and loyalty. The future of the concept of customer success has finally arrived, where it is now seen as the ultimate growth engine for businesses and a key differentiator for companies who are truly *"customer-centric"* in the way they think, act and function.

Original Recipe for The SaaS-y Customer Success Sauce

If you notice my definition of customer success above, I have used the word "strategy" rather than "function" or "department". It is because customer success does not start or end with hiring a customer success team or leader (though that is one of the non-negotiable components of your customer success journey). The concept of customer success is multi-dimensional and can be looked at in many ways, all of which point to the customer at the core of its definition, and a company-wide effort towards ensuring their success.

There are three components that go into making customer success a winning strategy for your organization: **experience**, **outcomes** and **value**.

Customer Success $=$ Experience $+$ Value $+$ Outcomes

These are the ingredients to the *"customer success secret sauce"* that will lead your customers to **stay** with you, **grow** with you and **rave** about you. It's what makes customer success so cool, and so important in the world of Software-as-a-service (SaaS), or any service that offers a subscription-based model. Let's explore each of them one by one:

Experience

The focus of companies big and small, in any industry, has shifted from just selling products and services to providing experiences that stick with the buyer throughout their journey and help maintain customer loyalty and advocacy. So, no matter what you do, you are in _"The business of experience"_.

Renowned American author B. Joseph Pine II, who coined the term _"experience economy"_, has said that _"An experience is not an amorphous construct; it is as real an offering as any service, good, or commodity."_ This experience stems from your interactions with customers, the way your product works, the way you capture and respond to their feedback - every single touchpoint, digital or in-person, contributes to this experience. Each time you engage with your customers, the connection should be a personal and memorable one.

Research shows that customer experience can be directly correlated to loyalty and better financial results. In a survey conducted in 2019, Qualtrics[2]

2   The State of Customer Experience Management, By Bruce Temkin, CCXP Head of the Qualtrics XM Institute Maggie Mead Research Associate July 2019

reports that sixty-one per cent of CX leaders said that they had seen better financial results than their competitors by investing in their customer experience program.

If your customers value their experience with you as much as the offering that they have purchased from you, then you need to put as much time and resources into making that experience seamless. The famous saying, *"People will forget what you said, but they'll remember how you made them feel"*, holds true in the business world as equally as it does in other areas of our lives.

Investing in a measurable, consistent and scalable customer experience strategy should be one of the key goals of a business.

Outcomes

An outcome is a tangible, measurable result or a set of results that your customers see after using your offering. Your customers invest in your product or service with a goal in mind, and how you help them achieve that goal differentiates you as a strategic partner as opposed to just a vendor who sells to them. Your customers' outcomes are always associated with funded initiatives that are usually defined by executive leadership in your customers' business and then broken down into steps and planned for execution by different cross-functional leaders and their teams. The use of your product is usually a part of these funded initiatives and is tied to the key goals of the customer's program of work.

Outcomes signify a clear "end state" when they are achieved, which may or may not be different from the customer's "desired state". That journey from the vision to practicality and then the reality of your customers' goals, identifying and addressing issues and pitfalls in the process, and subsequently being able to translate them into specific, measurable outputs, results in a true partnership that makes you their trusted advisor.

Value

Customer value is the "perceived worth" of your service or product to a customer, or in other words, the benefit your offering provides in comparison to your competitors. Understanding the concept of customer value is instrumental towards not only building a stronger, more trustworthy relationship with your existing customers but in attracting new ones too.

Value is very different from price, but price definitely contributes to the perceived value of your offering. This is because your customers' cost to use your product or service is more than just the price they pay you. There are other factors such as resources, time etc., that weigh into their perception of the benefit of using your solution instead of other similar ones available in the market.

Customer value takes into account several factors such as the innovation of your offering, criticality to your customer's business, your brand image, the effort that goes into buying, deploying and then learning to use your solution, and most importantly the benefit a customer receives in relation to the cost they incur.

Value comes not only from the functional aspect of what your product or service does for a customer, but also from what they experience while using it. The important thing to remember is that the process of showcasing value in your customer's journey is a continual one.

It is no secret that companies who put customer-centricity at the heart of their strategy win *hearts*, *minds* and *business*. If you are able to truly get the three ingredients of customer success right, you will be able to unlock the holy grail of growth strategies - "Customer-Led Growth"

Customer-Led Growth

Customer-Led Growth is a new approach to doing business that uses the power of customer insights and outcomes to achieve growth. In a customer-led growth strategy, the work of all departments, such as, product, sales and marketing is driven by a common understanding of what their customers' most favourable outcomes would be. As these outcomes are realized and value is delivered during different phases of the customer's journey, all your teams win, your customers wins, and ultimately your business wins.

The entire concept of customer-led growth is based on the premise that all functions within a company operate with a great customer experience as their most desirable outcome. But this is easier said than done! What has now been named one of the most proven strategies that will shape the future of SaaS businesses requires more than just an education on how customer success functions. Bringing about customer-led growth requires a shift in your company's culture, enabling points of customer feedback throughout their journey and using that feedback to drive retention, growth and new customer acquisition.

Being customer-led does not mean that you deprioritize your product or marketing effort. In fact, listening to the right customer feedback and knowing the needs and constraints of your customers will fuel your marketing and product-led growth. There is no reason why any combination of these growth models cannot co-exist. The idea behind product-led growth, for example, is that your product and the experience from that product help you attract, retain and expand your customer base. Complement this with a customer-led growth model, and the experience becomes more aligned to the users' needs, giving you increased retention and growth. Similarly, in a sales or marketing-led growth model, you rely on your marketing and sales teams to create a pipeline of revenue-generating customers. Combining this with a customer-led approach gives you users that not only buy from you, but stay and buy some more (and if you do it right, they bring their friends too!). The bottom line is that no matter what you do, focusing on a customer-led growth strategy is a must-have and a non-negotiable.

The journey to customer-led growth is defined by how closely you are able to tie the value and outcomes of your business to those of your customers' business. This is what drives your customers' buying decisions and is the reason why the growth strategies of some companies work better than others. It all starts with understanding how customer relationships work in the world of subscriptions and how you can leverage the power of those relationships to their full extent for mutual wins.

Chapter 2

GETTING THE RELATIONSHIP RIGHT

"Subscriptions are like marriages. It takes a lot of work to find the 'right' one; staying in a bad one is painful, and divorce could be costly!"

The professional relationship between a buyer and a seller is like any other human relationship, fueled by needs, thoughts and emotions. With the vast range of choices available in the market, it is equally hard to be a customer as it is to find one.

Finding a Customer: The Seller's Story

So you've got an amazing product, a world-class sales team, leads are pouring in, and converting into customers left, right and center. Sounds easy as ABC, but is it? Great companies spend a great deal of time, money and resources in putting their brand out in the market and in acquiring new customers.

Your Customer Acquisition Cost (CAC) is the sum of all costs incurred in marketing and lead generation efforts, employee salaries, costs of social activities such as prospect lunches and dinners, sales commissions once the deal is closed, and any other expenses that go into finding a new customer for your business for a given period, divided by the number of customers you acquire during that time.

Think of all the time, effort and money involved in putting your services and products out in the market and ensuring that they reach the right audience - all the advertising, the marketing collateral and publicity. How long have you spent spreading the word about your brand at online and in-person events, or following up with leads, trying to strike up a conversation that sparks people's interest? And don't forget the countless product demos, pitches and meetings you go through that may or may not convert into revenue for your business.

Quite a process, right? Now think about your buyer. Believe it or not, their journey of finding you is equally hard, if not harder.

Finding a Seller: The Journey of a Buyer

Buyers are smart; they know what they want and why they want it. They also know that for any given requirement, the choices are plentiful. That's why selling is not an easy job. What we have to understand here is that the process a buyer undergoes in reaching a set of requirements by clearly defining business objectives, and then going to market to find a partner that can deliver those needs is a long cycle that consumes time, money and resources too.

A company's hunt for a technology vendor or partner usually starts with a "core business need" or a "problem" that needs to be solved. This is then approved to be a funded initiative sponsored by the executive leadership team and broken down into a program of work to be carried out by departmental heads, leads and their teams. There is an intensive amount of work involved in defining the scope of the project, gathering stakeholder requirements, deciding the kind of technology that will be needed, and which vendors will be considered to be part of the process. There is a rigorous business analysis and documentation involved in getting all this done, and often, external consultants are brought in to lend their expertise to the process. This is even before potential vendors are shortlisted, and product demonstrations and pricing are requested.

Then comes the moment of truth, selecting the vendor they want to work with. A lot of factors contribute to this decision, such as:

- *Suitability*: product fit to business requirements, total cost of ownership, ease of implementation, ease of adoption, terms of the contract including ease of cancellation (yes, you read that right!)
- *Brand reputation*: Your brand's vision and mission, market leadership, references etc.

- *The sales experience*: The emotional experience of the sales process, such as display of empathy, understanding of their needs and personalization in the sales cycle, plays a huge part in a customer's decision.

(I want you to remember this process because a lot of the foundations for determining customer outcomes for success lie here)

The Value of Staying (or Leaving)

The setback involved in realizing that a technology partnership has not worked out during the course of a project is financially and emotionally draining for a customer. The process of selecting yet another vendor for the same purpose, the cost of migrating to another technology product or service, undergoing the change management process (which can be quite complicated, especially in larger organizations), and the time and cost involved in training their resources to adopt that technology all adds up to the massive delays and setbacks that a business experiences when their choice of vendor does not work out as expected and planned.

But as a provider, don't be drawn into thinking that customers will stick with you in fear of the effort that is required to undergo a change. If you are anything less than an ideal partner for them, any business would rather go through the entire buying cycle again to choose a new, more fit-to-purpose provider than be with one that doesn't serve their need to succeed.

The same is true on the seller's side; it can cost a company up to *nine* times more money to acquire a new customer than it takes to retain an existing one. And even after that, it can take a significant amount of time for a company to break even after customer acquisition, and it could be one or multiple renewals before the deal turns into a profit.

So, when you acquire a customer or become one, and you have to let go in the first year, it's a loss for everyone involved.

With all of these efforts from both parties, it only makes sense that we try and get the next steps right once we've selected a technology partner or won a customer (depending on what side of the equation you're on).

Churn & VOC Consultant Anita Toth very aptly compares the process of winning and losing a customer to dating, marriage and divorce. She says, *"Every customer's journey is a unique one and is filled with expectation and hope, and it is turned from possibility to reality in collaboration with the vendors and companies they work with."* When a customer decides to end this journey with you, it is extremely crucial to analyze how big the gap between their expectations of your company and the reality once they became a customer was. A customer's decision to leave or stay is underpinned by emotion and backed by rational evidence. And every step in their journey with you contributes to it."

Why Customers Churn

"It's not the price that's too high; it's the return on investment that's too low."

Churn or customer attrition is one of the most dreaded words for a company. Mathematically, churn can be calculated in a number of different ways. During any given period, churn could be:

- The number of customers you have lost (this is known as *logo churn* or *customer churn*)
- The total amount or percentage of recurring revenue lost (also known as *revenue churn*)

Irrespective of the way you measure it, churn is not a favourable outcome for your business, but it definitely could be a key learning. An important thing worth noting while measuring churn is that it is a lagging indicator because it only gives you something that has already happened. The events, or lack thereof, that contribute to a customer's churn start happening way before they actually inform you of their decision to part ways with your company and product. So, it is crucial for companies to look at their churn rate as an indicator of behaviour rather than just a number or percentage, and then to use it to ask important questions which can help analyze (and predict) why customers are leaving and what you can do to prevent it from happening. We'll look at this in further detail in Chapter 5.

Let's explore some of the most common reasons for customer churn:

- **Price**: Price is one of the main reasons customers provide when making the decision to end their subscription. Often, customers have departmental budget cuts that require them to scrap some external solutions, or a competitor may offer a similar or seemingly better solution at a better price, causing the customer to end their journey with you. When a customer feels the price is too high, it is generally an indication of the fact that the costs do not justify the benefit of using your product.

- **Change of strategy/personnel:** Companies often undergo re-organization, and your new point of contact or relationship owner may not have the same plans as the previous one. This change in direction could lead to a decision that involves not using your solution anymore. Sometimes, even when the strategic direction has not changed, your new relationship owner may replace your solution with another due to sheer personal preference.

Again, this points to the possible lack of buy-in from other stakeholders in the project, which can boil down to the fact that they did not see enough value in the solution to champion to continue using it in front of their new leadership. (though this may not always be the case, sometimes it really is the customer's strategy that changes and vendors have little to no influence over it)

- **Expectations not met**: Often, customers feel like a product does not meet their expectations once they start using it. This could be either due to the fact that it really doesn't fit their needs or they may not have had the help they needed in using it right. Either way, it leads to churn.

- **Time to first value**: Time to first value is the duration it takes for a customer to achieve their first practical outcome, or have their first "aha" moment with your product. If the time to first value is too long (this could be due to a long implementation cycle, lack of proper onboarding, gaps in understanding etc.), then the customer's uptake of the product will not be as expected, and it leads to churn. This is one of the cases where your product might end up being on the "unused technology" shelf before being scrapped.

- **Less than optimal experience**: A poor experience could be attributed to lack of quality support, onboarding and implementation, or faulty features and bugs in the product. Good service and experience are non-negotiables for customers. Remember that your competitors are also pitching their services to the market all the time, and if that comes with a better product and service than yours, customers will move away from your offering to someone who "does it better".

While this is not a definitive list of all the reasons that lead to churn, it gives you some of the most common ones. If you look at each of the points above, you will notice that most of them can be attributed to the lack of "perceived value" that we defined as a core component of customer success in Chapter 1.

When a customer loses sight of the full value you can provide to them, they are a flight risk. Your challenge, as a vendor here, is to know your customer well enough to know their current goals and also be deeply embedded into their strategy to have visibility into their future needs, and know what part you will play in their long term plans. It is also crucial to ensure that your clients understand the full breadth of what you offer as a company, even if they have only purchased a part of your offering at the time. As a business, you need to ensure that your customers understand the value of what you do for them - so you are not seen as a "nice to have" but an essential, and to be the supplier customers turn to, not away from. The best way to do this is to anticipate the customer's needs and ensure that you are consistently delivering, and most importantly, communicating value to several customer stakeholders, who may want to achieve different things using your product or service.

What Customers Want

We've just talked about why customers leave, and it is often because they don't get something they want, or because their expectations are not met. So, what is it that makes them stay with a company?

While building new products and services, companies take things such as industry trends, what other companies in a similar space are doing, and technological advancements into consideration. And while these are all great sources for assessing market need when your product is in development, your source of truth for determining the initial success and future roadmap of your product are your customers. Their decision to stick with you or opt for someone else at any point in their technology and digital transformation journey is determined by how good a fit you are for them.

Remember that customers buy from companies because they either have a problem or issue to address or business requirements that need to be fulfilled. That's what brings them to you, but beyond that fundamental reason is everything else that surrounds your product or service and makes it better, and that's what makes them stay.

Let's explore some of the biggest traits companies look for in their technology vendors and partners:

- **Innovation**
  Robert Iger, Former CEO and Chairman of The Walt Disney Company, pointed out, *"If you are not innovating, you're dying!"*

  If you are in the business of technology, then innovating is beyond just fixing bugs to make your product better. The world of SaaS is fiercely competitive and vendors are easily replaceable if they are not staying on top of their game. From the way your product evolves with changing market needs to the way you enhance your customers' experience and day-to-day interactions with your team and company makes a huge difference to their perception of you as a business. Customers' problems and goals are constantly evolving, and your product needs to keep up with those needs. Delve into the power of listening to your customers and gathering their feedback to fuel your innovation strategy. When your product regularly evolves to showcase features that customers felt were missing or things that make the product more intuitive, it enhances customer retention.

- **Communication**
  Customers expect to see transparency in the way you listen to them and communicate with them. And this extends beyond the human interactions you have with them to your digital channels too. Better communication leads to greater trust and better partnerships with your customers. For example, it is next to useless if you are constantly releasing new features but don't have an effective way of communicating those to your customers, or a way of gathering their feedback on those features and which new ones they'd like to see. Customers appreciate it when they are given opportunities to share feedback about their experience and interactions with your technology and your team, and knowing that their feedback is acknowledged and deemed valuable.

Additionally, it's crucial that you convey to your customers how you operate as a company and what you stand for. With companies sharing crucial data and business plans with their SaaS vendors, transparency in communicating how you handle customer information, your policies and how your company plans change and progress with your customers, goes a long way in keeping the relationship strong and steady.

- **Personalization**
Customers expect SaaS providers to offer customization and flexibility that helps make the solution work for them. This feeds into everything right from how product features are packaged together and priced, to how the end-user experience and communication is personalized. It also includes allowing room for growth as their user base on your platform grows, and all of this needs to be factored into the price you offer them.

- **Convenience**
Customers value convenience more than anything. Everybody leads busy lives, and people don't have an extra few minutes let alone hours or days to figure out stuff that seems even remotely complicated. Customers rely on external technology to save time, not to spend

more time learning and using it. Therefore, they prefer solutions that are easy to deploy, and easy to adopt for themselves and their team. Your product experience should be coupled with your adoption and education program in a way that it "fits like a glove" into your customers' operations. Most companies use a range of other technology solutions and expect them to speak to each other in order to make way for consistency in data and operations. So your product needs to have both off-the-shelf and custom integration options, and customers should have the option to be walked through and supported through these integrations in the form of an expert services offering that they are mostly happy to pay for additionally.

- **Emotion**
  A major factor that customers are driven by is emotion, and their sentiment towards you as a vendor is the foundation of the kind of loyalty that makes them stay forever. If a customer's loyalty is driven just by product features and convenience, then it's harder to maintain. Loyalty fueled by emotion, on the other hand, is harder to create but is what produces raving fans

  Brands that make visible efforts to showcase that they value their customers and learn their feelings, beliefs, wants and needs win. It is important that your customers feel a sense of authenticity in your interactions, both human and digital. Empowering your teams and technology to fulfil the need for ingenuity and authenticity is key.

"All the reasons for churn translate into lack of perceived value; all that customers want in order to stay is incremental value. If you don't give your customers the time, value and attention they need, someone else will!"

The Perfect Marriage: A Great Customer and Business that understands the True Value of Customer-centricity

Building a truly customer-centric approach guarantees a high potential for growth and sets your company up for success. Organizations are increasingly shifting their focus to adopting a customer-obsessed approach in addition to having a great product in order to gain a competitive edge in the market. Customer-centric companies are known to be more profitable than their competitors as they have an enhanced ability to retain their customers and attract new ones. This comes from high customer loyalty fueled by increased customer satisfaction, experience, success and service.

Gartner defines customer-centricity as:

"The ability of people in an organization to understand customers' situations, perceptions, and expectations. Customer-centricity demands that the customer is the focal point of all decisions related to delivering products, services and experiences to create customer satisfaction, loyalty and advocacy."

- ***Customer-centricity starts with knowing your customer:*** Being customer-centric means knowing, acknowledging and understanding the similarities and differences between your customers, their behaviours, preferences, needs and goals; and then using this information to drive your strategy and engagement plans.

  Empathy is one of the core principles of a customer-centric culture. It comes from understanding the true motivations and feelings of your customers, and understanding their psychology to unlock advantages for yourself and for your customers' businesses. Companies that are truly able to operationalize customer empathy not only know how to understand their customers needs and the reasons behind them, but also how to respond to them in the right way.

- *Customer-centricity requires a cultural shift:* A lot of companies unknowingly underestimate the value of an internal shift in culture that is required in their journey towards customer-centricity. In fact, this could be the main reason that most companies fail to deliver a compelling customer success model. Thinking and operating in silos can help you excel at certain kinds of interactions and maybe some customer outcomes, but it does not lead to a fuller, more holistic approach to customer-centricity.

- *Customer-centricity is different from being customer-focused:* There is a difference between being customer-focused (dealing with wants) and being customer-centric (dealing with needs). Companies that are truly customer-centric try to see the world from their customers' point of view.

- *Customer-centricity is not seen by the customer, but it is felt by them:* Your customers don't want to understand how your internal operations are organized, so your customer-centricity focus should go beyond marketing speak. You really need to "walk the talk" and the subsequent positive effects of that will show in the way your customers' needs are met with efficiency and how success is achieved in their outcomes and goals.

All the above translates into the importance of understanding your customers' needs to deliver a consistent experience and ongoing success as the customer moves into different phases of their journey with you. Ensuring you meet and exceed the expectations customers have of your brand, and that they are successful in their journey with you requires defining how you build customer-centricity into the way you function as an organization.

And that simply cannot be done by one department alone. In order for your organization to be truly customer-centric, customer success should be the responsibility of each and every department in your organization.

Chapter 3

CUSTOMER SUCCESS IS EVERYONE'S BUSINESS

"No one can whistle a symphony. It takes a whole orchestra to play it."

- H.E. Luccock

Let's say you are baking a cake (or replace the cake with your favourite dessert to fuel your imagination). You will go and shop for the best quality ingredients according to your budget, add them together in the right proportions and then use a whisk to bring everything together before baking it into the final product.

Now imagine this: If the success of your customers were a cake, then the work of all departments such as product, sales, marketing etc., are the ingredients that go into the cake, and your customer success function is the whisk that brings everything together into one wholesome, consistent and delightful customer experience. The ingredients, their quality and proportions are key to the taste of your cake. You can't have too much sugar with less flour, just like you can't have a great product with a weak sales team or vice versa. The timing, proportions and the role of each ingredient contributes to the quality of your cake, just like each department within your company plays a part in adding value to the journey of your customers.

Needless to say, while the accountability of making customers happy and successful is placed in the able hands of your customer success team, part of the responsibility lies with each and every other department within your company. Customer success is not a function or a job role; it is a mindset, a philosophy that needs to be embedded in how we work and how we function as a company.

The math is quite simple, if your customers succeed using your products and services, they will continue to use them and will stay with you. But here's where it gets complicated - building the system that leads to customers being successful with your offerings is an equation that involves the effort of your people, the consistency and design of your processes, and the way you collect and use data. Your customer success team then helps you bring it all together, and pave the way for customers to succeed. And one or more of these areas is where most organizations would get it wrong, or just lack consistency in the way they do things.

Your work is not done by just hiring a few customer success managers and creating a customer success function. That's where your journey starts.

Being a truly customer-obsessed organization starts with having a customer success function, and is fueled by the continual work of all other departments. And the work of leaders is to enable all roles and functions to help the customer success function drive success by building your customers' success metrics into the KPIs (key performance indicators) of your entire company.

Defining Your Organization-Wide Customer Success Narartive

The sales mantra to success is *"Always be closing"*. The ABC of Customer Success is *"Always be customer-centric"*. That should be your top-line mantra to positively impact your bottom-line.

Having an organization-wide vision and mission for customer success in your journey towards customer-centricity will require you to define what customer success means to your business, something that is unique to your offering and to your customers' needs. Customers in general may have the same requirements in terms of a quality product, great service and ease of use, but beyond all of this, their needs differ greatly. In the process of defining the fundamentals of your customer success strategy, it is crucial to ask questions like:

- What is unique about my customers and their businesses?

- What is the fundamental need that my offering serves?

- What is the first "wow" moment for my customers while using my product or service?

- What is the role my teams play in helping create the first and many more "wow" moments for my customers' businesses?

The answers to these questions will pave your path forward.

The Customer-centricity Charter: *Make Customer Success Your PRIDE*

The fundamentals of developing a customer success mindset for your entire company are not hard to apply, but it takes a conscious, consistent, and continual effort for them to be truly embedded into your people, processes and product. A culture is built using a combination of values and behaviours, and that holds equally true for the culture of customer-centricity. Your journey towards customer success starts with connecting the goals and priorities of your business to the goals and priorities of your customers, and then building that connection into your culture by creating a constant awareness within every individual in the organization and enabling them to perform in a way that upholds that culture in everything they do at work.

Let's look at the 5-step process to make customer success your **PRIDE**:

- **P**rioritize the purpose
- **R**eflect on your current state
- **I**ncentivize
- **D**iscover your customers' needs
- **E**ducate and Engage Continually

| Prioritize | Reflect | Incentivize | Discover | Educate & Engage |

Make Customer Success your PRIDE

Let's unpack these one by one:

Prioritize the Purpose

Making customer success a company-wide priority starts with leadership understanding and buy-in. A clearly articulated vision detailing what customer success and centricity mean to your business is a critical step in your journey. Your customer success leader will be accountable for the overall strategy but in order to take the right steps for embedding it as a culture, leaders need to lead by example from the top, with executives owning key parts of the customer journey, and then the senior management using their leadership to drive customer-centricity within their teams.

While establishing the vision and steps for your customer success strategy, it is crucial to know that it's not just about focusing on the goals of your strategy, but also on the inspiration behind the goals; the WHY! And then translate this into specific activities and actions that people need to start doing and keep doing. This will help clarify what specific roles and outcomes are expected of each team and how it ties into the bigger picture. Remember that even if each department is thinking about the customer but doing it in silos, it won't get you very far; they must also be able to understand the input and impact of others in the organization on customer success, and how they can not only help the customer but their colleagues in other teams as well. It has been truly pointed out by several experts that "Customer Success is a team sport", and while it might be almost wishful to have all departments within a company working in complete synchronization, it is possible to enable them in a way that they are able to work in close collaboration with one another to achieve the common goal of being customer-centric.

Your people will need help in understanding the roles they play in your customer success strategy, and how they can take a more customer-centric approach to their job. Some of them may need more help than others, and it is important that they know that their learning and development is supported and guided by leadership. Your people are the most crucial component in the execution of your customer-centric approach and coaching them and building their confidence in the process will require continued commitment from leadership.

Reflect on your Current State

Where you are starting on the journey is as important as where you would like to get to. Having clear sight of how much work needs to be done with your people, processes and culture is key to having a pragmatic approach to customer-centricity. An analysis of your current state will also give you sight of the operational metrics, indicative cost and risks associated with your strategy, which you can use to feed into the goals and activities of your working plan for each department.

Your team's thoughts and ideas are a key contribution to your actions and strategy. Seeking input from teams who play different roles in the customer's journey will not only give you the chance to hear real examples of your customers' pain points but also in addressing any gaps that hinder your people from doing their roles in the best possible way. Your frontline teams are the first to feel the effect of customer unhappiness and issues, so they will not only tell you what those issues are but also what internal processes and systems can be improved to avoid those problems in future. Get feedback from all functions on what they're missing to fill out the white space in their understanding of customer success and how it's relevant to their role. This could be a simple brainstorming session with all leaders meeting their teams to gather feedback and then regrouping with other leaders to build a plan of action. Customer success leadership circles chaired by customer success leadership and including leaders and representatives from all other areas of the business could be an effective way to start and continually improve on the idea of "Customer Success as a Culture."

Incentivize

Building formal and informal incentives for employees based on their commitment and focus towards customer success is a great way to drive your strategy forward. It motivates people to strive to do their best and also allows leadership to measure the impact of individual and departmental performance on your overall strategy.

Each department can have shared metrics for customer success tied to their KPIs, and individual metrics based on their roles. For example, NPS (Net

Promoter Score) can be a shared metric between Account Management, Customer Success and Product teams. Similarly, retention metrics can be shared between teams too (we'll dive into the detail of specific metrics in Chapters 5 and 6). Some companies also offer bonuses or cash incentives based on the business' revenue performance and metrics related to customer retention. This encourages staff to be committed towards understanding and delivering customer impact.

Again, the way you do this is going to depend on how your organization is structured and how you want to establish shared accountabilities between departments, but establishing the basic metrics and benchmarks for achievement is a good starting point for building customer-centricity as an expectation from your employees, and also adding an element of risk that comes with not having a customer-centric attitude.

Apart from KPIs and bonuses, recognition is also a powerful tool to motivate people. I've worked for a company in the past that would announce great customer feedback for different teams in their All Hands meetings. These emails, or customer responses on tickets or other systems would be read by the CEO with a recognition of the employee who the feedback was meant for. It was a great motivator for employees to go above and beyond in helping customers at all times.

Formal compensation and recognition plans combined will give you a great way to establish and quantify the relationship between your company's customer-centric culture and the impact it has on your customers' success.

Discover your Customers' Needs

A customer-centric culture comes from understanding your customers, and this goes beyond knowing what they buy from you and how much they pay you. True business intelligence for customer success is fueled by customer data and it gives your team the insights and knowledge they need to deliver exceptional value in their everyday conversations with customers.

We will cover customer data and health metrics in much greater detail in Chapter 5, but some of the main reasons that a lot of companies struggle in getting their customer success and centricity strategy right are either due to lack of the right data points, or the lack of the right tools and processes to use that data to segment and target customers.

Customer feedback is another powerful form of insights and value, and can be collected through digital channels such as emails and surveys or in conversations with executives and frontline teams. We will uncover the value and strategy for effectively collecting and responding to customer feedback in Chapter 6.

Aside from using the data and feedback metrics to fuel your teams' conversations and interactions with customers, equipping them with knowledge about how customers operate and their business sector or industry allows them to position themselves in a way that showcases a deeper commitment to making customers successful. I remember one time when I was talking to a customer and they shared a challenge they had been facing that they weren't able to secure funding for the business. It immediately reminded me of an article I had read talking about a government grant for a similar program and I was able to point my customer in that direction. They were elated and thankful, and though it wouldn't have mattered even if I didn't have a solution to the problem they described as it had nothing to do with the service my company was providing, having knowledge of the sector and recent developments and happenings helped take the conversation to the next level.

Equipping your team with knowledge about your customers and the industries they work in enables creative problem solving that helps build the foundation for long-term relationships. We will revisit the art of customer conversations in greater detail in Chapter 7.

Educate and Engage Continually

Your journey towards building a customer-centric culture is long and also never-ending. It is something that needs constant effort and action for continued excellence and sustainable results.

So your customer-centricity focus doesn't dwindle away in the midst of evolving priorities and newer projects, sharing your vision and purpose continually with your team will help them keep it on top of mind.

Creating a system that allows you to constantly measure and articulate the impact of your employees on customer-centricity and the value it brings to your customers and your business gives you a chance to celebrate successes and also transparently highlight gaps and discover areas of improvement. Shared KPIs and shared accountability can be fueled by benchmarking your metrics so that all departments can streamline their performance.

Continuous improvement should always be a part of your plan and training your employees, both new and existing ones, is key to keeping the momentum going. It helps reinforce what they have learnt and encourages them to use it in their daily activities. This ongoing coaching can be delivered via departmental leaders and through the use of content in your employee enablement program. Have them take a customer-centricity assessment each quarter just like you give them one for IT, Human Resources and Cybersecurity related policies. You can also use surveys to gauge the usefulness of customer-centricity training and tailor content based on feedback.

Aligning your company's working culture with your customer success strategy will help you support your vision and pave the way forward for the success of your employees, your customers and ultimately, your business.

Heidi Rhodes, Director of Global Enterprise Customer Experience at Cisco says,

"One of the biggest mistakes well-intentioned companies make is believing that having a customer success team means that they are a customer-centric company. It does not. Being truly customer-centric means creating a customer feedback loop, listening regularly to customers, and committing to prioritize investment in activities that meet their customers' needs. Customer-centricity starts with senior leadership team commitment to their customers' success. Once gaps and opportunities are identified in a customer's

journey, cross-functional alignment and prioritization is needed to drive action.

If they commit, step number one is investing in a formal customer journey mapping capability. This is not only a 'CS team thing.' Many different organizations within a company impact or own a part of the customer's journey. Creating a proper customer journey map allows your company to have a "gut-check" on the experience they are providing across the board.

The second biggest mistake companies make is believing that their outcome and their customers' outcome are the same thing. Of course, the more successful your customers are, the more your business grows. But success and outcomes are two very different things.

Sometimes, being a customer-centric company looks like the CSM teams driving internal alignment on priorities and being an advocate for your customers when they can't be in the room.

So, do you need a Customer Success Team to be a customer-centric company? Yes.

Is that enough? No."

The Role of your Teams in Customer Success

Customer-centric organizations do not work in silos; each department and each employee has their own role to play in the engagement of customers and in cross-functional collaboration. As such, a connected employee experience and employee success is a must-have in order to achieve best-in-class customer success. Happy customers come from the efforts of happy employees. Motivated people who feel fulfilled with the work they do and know that their endeavours are supported by peers and leaders reflect that positivity and enthusiasm about your business in customer conversations. Before you can build championship and advocacy with customers, your people need to be the biggest champions and supporters of everything you do and stand for as a business.

Why? Because your employees are technically your first "customers" and they signed up to believe in your vision when they started to work for you, and in order to ensure that connection stays strong, you need to focus on their success, just the way you would for your customers. Employee success, advocacy and value is built on the foundations of empathy, support from leadership, appreciation and recognition. A supportive workplace helps your employees be more confident in the way they build positive experiences with customers and that drives stronger loyalty for everyone. And while there could be a whole other book on employee experience, what I want to highlight here is that a conversation about being customer-centric goes hand in hand with being people-centric; you cannot afford to exclude any one of these in your growth plans as a business.

With that very important point made, let's explore the roles different functions play in your journey towards customer-centricity.

Marketing

Marketers help shape your messaging to your existing customers and potential ones. Their skills in understanding and communicating your value proposition makes them a resource to help fuel retention and growth in addition to driving your customer acquisition efforts. For many businesses, the start of a great experience for customers is through the work of the marketing team. But more often than not, marketing efforts are too disconnected from the work of customer success, and that lack of consistency can lead to a huge gap in the reality of the experience provided to your customers. In order to bridge this gap, now most companies have an established function dedicated to customer marketing in their journey towards providing best-in-class value and success to their customers. This team focuses on meaningful and valuable account-based experiences that drive retention and growth.

Sales

Your sales team is the first human interaction your customers have with your business. Empowering your sales team to be great "closers" also implies empowering them to be great listeners. When sales teams unlock goals and key needs of the customer in their interactions, they sign up customers that stay, and by passing on the details of their conversations to other teams that interact with the customer after the sale, the sales team paves the way for long-term success for everyone.

Customer Service

One of the key measures of satisfaction for your business is the way you deal with your customers' issues. The times when something doesn't work or customers run into a problem are key moments in your customers' journey with you, and the way you help them through those times greatly affects their perception of your business. Your customer support team's interaction amplifies this satisfaction through prompt, valuable responses and understanding your customers' needs.

Product

A closely-tied relationship between product and customer success teams keeps the flow of ideas and growth going. As the success team guides internal teams towards customer needs, it fuels the aim of the product team, which is to understand end users better and deliver solutions and product features that evolve with changing needs. Customer-centric organizations often have product leaders actively participating in Customer Advisory Boards (more on this in Chapter 6), along with their customer success leaders to effectively gauge customers' needs and use that to influence the product and service roadmap in close alignment with the company's mission.

Information Technology

Your IT function is uniquely positioned to influence your customers' success. They do this by creating synergy between all the tools and technology you use internally and for customer-facing activities. They also set policies for security and data collection, all of which have a significant impact on the success of your customers.

Human Resources

Your Human Resources department helps maintain continued alignment between your employees, their performance and benefits with your customer-centricity vision. They also help with hiring the right workforce and onboarding and training them as per your company and customer values. Your HR team are the true "internal promoters" of the value of customer success and customer-centricity.

Customer Success

Let's talk about the function that brings all of the great work done by everyone else in the company together - your customer success department a.k.a "The Whisk". Externally, your customer success team advocates for the customers, understanding their needs and goals and aligning with them closely to drive outcomes and maximize value. They listen to your customers continually, drive their strategy forward and unlock maximum value for the customer using your product or service. Internally, they drive cross-functional efforts to ensure each team has the most up-to-date information they need in order to do their roles in the best possible capacity to drive growth and success for customers. They bridge the gap between customers' needs and value delivered to fuel the growth of your business and turn customers into raving fans.

Experts and leaders have often stated that customer success is "not" support or sales. While that is absolutely true, what's important to understand is that while the customer success "department" is not any of these things, *All your other departments are customer success*. When your teams understand the very important roles they each play in driving business growth through creating value and meaningful experiences for your customers, you can start to build a customer journey that has success weaved into each and every phase.

Part II: Build, Measure and Execute

Chapter 4
BUILDING SUCCESS FROM PROPOSAL TO RENEWAL

My husband and I took a trip to the beautiful country of Mauritius a few years ago. The first three days of the trip were supposed to be a guided tour followed by the next few that left room for self-exploration. We landed in this beautiful place full of beaches, great food and the most amazing cultural scene, but I didn't particularly enjoy the first few days of my holiday. Because the guided tour didn't cover visits to any of the places I would've liked. It wasn't uninteresting or bad, it just wasn't what I would've "loved" to do on the majority of my holiday. That changed when we spent the next few days with a local friend who asked us where we wanted to go and took us to explore some of the most amazing spots and sample the best food and culture the place had to offer. The experience was surreal, and I enjoyed every single second because it was built around "what I loved".

Moral of the story: Not everything works for everyone, especially when you want them to have a great experience and not an average one.

So, my question to you is *"Do you know what your customer's world looks like? And where do you fit in that world?"*

If you're taking a journey with them, and wish for that journey to be a rewarding and successful one, remember to make your customer the hero of the story and build the strategy of your partnership with them around that. The journey will decide the difference between *"It's all right, does what it needs to do"*, and *"It's great, I'm very happy and will bring my friends to try it."*

Customer-led journeys begin with the customer, and even though it is crucial to incorporate facets of how your business wins and profits from making that journey successful, most businesses forget the customer part of the journey, and that's where it goes wrong. Making assumptions about the customer and designing your journey based on that is a recipe for failure at worst and mediocrity at best. And it's not enough to just shed your assumptions, it is equally important to understand the goals and motivation behind everything your customers do.

Things to remember while designing your customer-led journey:

- Your journey should be driven by the customer's intent in order for it to be relevant to their goals

- Customer journeys are unique, depending on their needs. Even in the same business, the priorities of individual stakeholders can vary
- Customer journeys are non-linear; allow for flexibility to accommodate unforeseen changes to your ideal scenarios
- Consistency is key through different phases of the journey. Salesforce's *State of the connected customer report*[3] states that *"Fifty-four percent of customers say it generally feels like sales, service, and marketing don't share information."*

Even though customer success teams are designed to start functioning after a customer signs up i.e. the sale has been made, your customer's success journey starts the moment you have your first sales interaction with them. Different teams own the journey at different points, so if consistency of transition and flow of information and ownership at each stage is not clearly defined, your customer's experience during the journey will be broken. As your team navigates the customers through their unique needs, a connected experience makes the journey seamless for everyone involved. But this is where most companies tend to be disconnected.

In this chapter, we'll explore how you can enable your teams to view the customer journey from the viewpoint

---

3   Salesforce State of the Connected Customer, 4th Edition

of both your business and the customer's and operate in a way that offers consistency, collaboration and mutual growth.

The content of this chapter is divided into the four key phases in a customer's journey with a business, the considerations, and the solutions for success to help make memorable moments for your customer in each of these phases:

- *Acquisition*
- *Value Realization*
- *Value Expansion*
- *Renewal & Advocacy*

	What It Means	
	To You	**To Your Customers**
Acquisition	Creating a revenue-generating customer.	Selecting a partner that will help them successfully realize their goals
Value Realization	Onboarding and training users; regular meetings and reviews to help them stay on track; supporting and guiding the customer with any help they need	Spending time on learning how to use a new system; training their teams; and then having their first "aha" moment when your product helps them hit a goal, or starts to show real value for the first time.
Value Expansion	Expanding the revenue potential of an existing customer	The realization that they can do so much more with your product and it can add value to more of their business process than they had initially thought.
Renewal & Advocacy	Retaining a customer and gaining a loyal advocate for your business, and continually putting in the work needed to maintain that advocacy.	Realizing the full value of their partnership with you, investing in their future with your business and becoming true believers in the offerings you provide.

Table: Your customers' lifecycle from their perspective and yours

Acquisition

What it Means

- *To you: Creating a revenue-generating customer.*

- *To the customer: Selecting a partner that will help them successfully realize their goals*

"Don't let the pizza be too different from the picture"

You're hungry and come across a social media advertisement with a picture of the most scrumptious looking pizza. So you pick up the phone and try to order it online, only to be put on hold by the store for a few minutes, or you try to do a web order but the website isn't very friendly. Anyway, you somehow muster up the patience to place that order because it seems worth going through a tiny bit of trouble for the most delicious-looking pizza ever made. The doorbell rings as you're dreaming of a hot and delicious bite of pure heaven, only for you to witness a lukewarm cheese pie that looks nowhere close to the picture you had seen. This is what I call the "appetite crusher", better known in the corporate world as the "value gap". When the perceived value of your product or service is very different from the actual value it delivers to the customer after purchase, it leads to dissatisfaction and ultimately churn.

The first step in addressing the value gap is to clearly outline value during the acquisition phase of your customer's lifecycle. When a customer enters your sales cycle, they start exploring the basics of what you do in general, but don't know much about what your product or service can do for them. That's when your sales team holds their hands and strategically navigates through the process of how your offering is the right fit to help them achieve their goals. Your customers share a lot of information about their pain points, plans and areas for improvement during this time, and the aim should be to help them understand how your product helps them achieve those goals and overcome those pain points, and to help customers with "solutions" not "products".

Salesforce's *State of the Connected Customer* report puts the spotlight on how B2B relationships are falling short of buyer expectations due to *"failure to demonstrate an understanding of a buyer's unique circumstances, which causes sales representatives to push products rather than solutions"*. The report shows that:

- 57% of business buyers feel that sales representatives often lack adequate knowledge of their business,
- 63% of them focus on pushing products rather than solutions to business problems, and

- 73% of them feel that most sales interactions feel transactional.

The statistics above highlight the importance of building customer-centricity into your acquisition strategy so that you not only acquire the right kind of customers that yield higher value for your business in the long run, but also start building trust and experience into the customer's journey right from the start. With the market shifting heavily towards customer-led growth, the sales motion needs to evolve too to enable more continuity between the prospecting, acquisition and retention processes. The knowledge and importance of understanding the customer's needs deeply and working your sales pitch to cover all of those needs will transform the buying experience and make it more meaningful to both parties.

Often, a high churn rate is an indication of a gap in your acquisition efforts. "Bad fit" customers are more prone to leaving when they find a better solution or realize that yours doesn't fulfil their needs. Value in the partnership works both ways; if you bring in the right customers, they will provide as much value to you as you do to them.

How to make your customer's Acquisition Journey meaningful:

1. *Know who your customers are*
   Every company exists for a reason; they solve a problem or fill a gap for their target customers. Most companies will equip their sales team with the power of their product and service, but often do not stress enough on why they do it and who they do it for. Helping your sales teams understand who your ideal customers are and also the personas of your buyers are the best way to get them to ask the right questions and dig deeper to make a connection between their prospects' needs and the unique value proposition of your product.

   Ideal Customer Profile

   Simply put, your ideal customer profile outlines the type of company that will be the best fit for your products and services. Now the most natural question to come to mind is, do you only sell to those who fit this profile?

   The answer is no.

   Your Ideal customer profile (ICP) is used to gauge your prospects and see which ones could be your most valuable and high potential customers in the future. Ideal customer profiles are built through leadership input and intense quantitative and qualitative analysis and include various data points, which could vary from company to company and the product or service they sell. This is different to your total addressable market or target customers, who will also be a valuable part of your prospecting, sales and success cycles and could end up being very valuable accounts too.

Knowledge of your ideal customer profile helps your marketing team with better targeting and faster sales cycles that win you accounts with potential higher lifetime value if they are nurtured in the right way once the sale has been made.

Buyer Personas

Hubspot defines buyer personas as *"Semi-fictional representations of your ideal customers based on data and research. They help you focus your time on qualified prospects, guide product development to suit the needs of your target customers, and align all work across your organization (from marketing to sales to service)"*

Your buyer personas include details of who buys from you, their behaviours, pain points etc. and this knowledge helps your sales team be better prepared for conversations with prospects (though this doesn't mean making assumptions based on the information in the personas, it means using the information to add value to your discovery and closing process)

2. **Why do customers buy from you and what causes them to go elsewhere?**
   Again, people buy because they have a "Why" (their business problem) and they choose a certain company over all the others in the mix because of several reasons such as how well their problem was understood, your competitive advantage, ease of buying, the sales experience etc. You need to identify these reasons and feed them into your sales enablement program. The same goes for reasons you lose deals and equipping your team with those learnings.

Knowledge of your customers' motivations, anxieties, outcomes coupled with your Unique Value Proposition (UVP), is a killer combination for success in the acquisition cycle for you and for your customers.

3. **How can you make it easier for them to do business with you?**

   Analysis of your customer-led acquisition funnel to identify points where buyers drop off in their journey creates a continual improvement process. So, is it your website, the journey from visit to enquiry, or the actual interaction with your sales team - the point where leads and prospects quit the buying cycle are opportunities for learning and improvement to enable a seamless way for your prospective customers to do business with you.

4. **How can you add value to the teams that help your buyers after the sale is made?**

   Three words: A clear handoff. Passing on critical information captured during the sales cycle sets your company and your customers up for success. All the information your prospects share about their pain points, plans and areas for improvement during the sales discovery process should form a part of their transition information once they become customers and are passed on to the hands of the next teams who interact with them during the rest of their journey.

   Account plans are the perfect tool for passing on this information to teams, such as customer success and account management that take carriage of the account after the sales cycle is complete. And these don't have to be too complicated or time-consuming. A simple one-pager capturing key stakeholders, key goals, buying motivation and dynamics, threats and expansion opportunities is a simple yet effective recipe for an account plan for your internal account transition meetings that complement the documentation. We discuss account plans in more detail in Chapter 7.

Value Realization

What it Means

- *To you: Onboarding and training users; regular meetings and reviews to help them stay on track; supporting and guiding the customer with any help they need.*

- *To customers: Spending time on learning how to use a new system, training their teams; and then having their first "aha" moment when your product helps them hit a goal, or starts to show real value for the first time.*

Once a customer signs up and starts their journey with you, you enter into the value realization phase. This includes their deployment or implementation cycle (if your product has one), onboarding, ongoing education, adoption and reviews and checkpoints in their journey. This is the longest phase of the cycle, and also the one that is full of opportunities to create memorable moments and wins for the customer.

How to Make Your Customer's Value Realization Journey Meaningful:

1. *A killer onboarding program*
   According to a 2022 research by Qualtrics, 30% of customers wish to see more "ease of use" in their products and services.

   This may not necessarily be a reflection of how complicated your product is (unless you have this specific repeated feedback from your key customers).

   In most cases, it reflects an onboarding and adoption problem. Most users are overwhelmed by the many things they see or hear during the onboarding phase. A good onboarding experience is so much more than just "training" end-users of your product. Onboarding is an entire program encompassing everything from that first welcome email to guidance in setting up the product, your knowledge base for new starters, the digital or in-person training sessions, and understanding and validating your customers' key objectives and priorities during this process.

Helping users focus on the areas of your product that are most meaningful to them, to help them get started on the right foot, and then help them uncover other functionalities as they become advanced users. This is the quickest way for you to help your customers have their first "aha" moment using your product. Make use of user personas to tailor your onboarding program and help customers extract maximum value.

Complementing your in-person training program with digital touchpoints such as in-app walkthroughs when users log in for the first time, and feature callouts (in-app or email-led) as the user starts their setup and usage journey really help accelerate adoption, and as your customers reach these little milestones in their adoption journey, don't forget to remind them that each thing they do with your product brings them one step closer to the goals they want to achieve. After all, it's the small wins that lead to big rewards!

2. **Account segmentation**
   Imagine yourself as a buyer. Would you like to be known as person X who purchased Y dollars

worth of items? We know what your answer to that is! It takes so much more to know what your customers are really about, and that is why multi-dimensional customer segmentation goes beyond just sorting your customers by revenue.

Segmentation is a powerful tool to equip your sales, customer success, marketing and product teams to get to know your customers better. It highlights behaviours, differences, commonalities, all of which feed into your digital and in-person interactions with them, and fuel the success and experience of your customers.

A good customer segmentation strategy is a foundational step towards success, and differs from company to company. It requires a thought process that considers the "why" and the "how" of the outcome you want to achieve from segmentation. So the first step is to determine what those customer segments are going to be. In addition to revenue, industry, demography, and geography, you can also include common elements of opportunity, risk, value and outcomes into your segments.

Once your baseline segments have been defined, use the combined effort of different teams that interact with the customers to help decide which segments they fall into. Also, remember that your customers will shift across some of the behavioural and qualitative segments during the course of their journey and your interactions with them will need to evolve as this happens.

3. **Meaningful touchpoints**

   Your interactions with your customers once they have completed a quality onboarding process define how value is realized using your product and how that leads to renewals, growth and advocacy. And no, "just checking in" doesn't quite cut it.

   Meaningful touchpoints with your customers should be aimed at clearly articulating the work you have collectively done, and how it feeds into their goals and outcomes. This can be achieved using a combination of in-person and digital interactions (more on the digital bit in Chapter 8 where we talk about personalized interactions at scale).

   Your segmentation strategy also feeds into the information you convey in these touchpoints, so do your account plans for your key accounts. The bottom line is that each touchpoint with your customers demands planning amongst teams, and most importantly, leaves lots of room to listen to them, and what they want to hear from you. If every meeting you have with them becomes a "what's going, not much" followed by a flurry of information from your side, most of which the customer will forget, it's not a productive conversation for anyone involved.

Our calendars are full, time is limited and there is so much to say. Think about what your customers want to hear and let them speak first to make way for meaningful meetings that everyone looks forward to (more on the art of customer conversations in Chapter 7).

The same goes for digital interactions. A customer once told me that they are annoyed by the repeated popups in their product, especially when they keep appearing while they're trying to look for some urgent reports. This is not an interaction, this is an "interference". Something similar happened with emails; a customer missed an important email from our company because there were just so many of them that they created a filter that put them in a folder they never accessed. Two examples that tell you a lot about important information getting lost in noise and the importance of focusing on quality and relevance in your interactions with your customers for continued success.

Value Expansion

What it Means

- *To you: Expanding the revenue potential of an existing customers*

- *To your customers: The realization that they can do so much more with your product and it can add value to more of their business process than they had initially thought.*

Having customers interested in buying more from you is a good indication of the value of the work you have done for them. Yet, cross-sell and up-sell conversations are ones that are often dealt with in the wrong way. However, when executed well, solid expansion interactions could be some of your best conversations with your customers. They pave the way for a chance to share the full breadth of what your solution offers, active engagement, a better understanding of needs beyond what you currently serve using your product and ultimately leads to stronger relationships.

An important thing we need to address about value expansion for your customers is the ownership of this stage of their lifecycle. Even though the accountability for this phase of the customer journey lies with account management and customer success teams, there is no single team that is responsible for expansion. These efforts could come from other departments such as marketing or a combined value-driven program from sales, marketing and customer success. Again, knowing where your customer is in their journey and having a common understanding of that between different departments is key to identifying and positioning a new offering or an upgrade in front of the customer.

How to Make Your Customer's Value Expansion Journey Meaningful:

1. **Position your offering in the right way, to the right person, at the right time**

   Due diligence is very important to the success of your expansion motion, as is flexible pricing and contracts to allow customers easy movement to a higher tier or additional offering. While upsell opportunities create room for a more feature-rich or "premium" version of your product and are indicative of your customers' business growth, creating the need for more features or licences, a cross-sell motion indicates the expansion of your business into other areas of your customer's business. As you can see, both of these call for very different approaches and positioning yourself to the right stakeholders at the right time with a flawless pitch that displays a strong understanding of their needs and how they will be fulfilled is a must-have. Cross-sell motions often involve selling to a different area of the business, so clearly articulating the value of what you're positioning to the right stakeholder is important.

2. **Foster the spirit of partnership**
   Positioning unused features or new features that don't fit into your customers' needs and goals bucket, hoping that they will buy them is not a great approach (clearly!). That doesn't mean you don't educate your clients about new or enhanced offerings, just do it keeping in mind the spirit of partnership that has brought you this far along.

   There have been multiple instances where I have seen account teams "strongly" pitching the shiny new premium feature or new product to a customer as part of a business review or regular catchup even when the customer is trying to gently nudge them away. This creates friction and a huge risk to your existing positioning and value too. Life is busy and no one needs a pushy sales pitch for something they don't need. So, clearly knowing the difference between "soft education and awareness to generate interest" and "strongly pushing new features and products" is important. Upselling and cross-selling takes understanding, thoughtfulness and planning for great execution to happen.

3. **Create natural curiosity through in-product experiences**
   Contextual communications through the product are a great way to drive expansion engagements digitally, given they are done at the right points in the customer's journey. Showcasing the benefits of an additional offering, or an upgrade or add-on at the right time, generates a high level of interest.

   I used to work for a company that offered cyber security solutions, and they landed their new offerings through in-product pop-ups and upgrade options redirecting people to their account teams for demos when they'd see a major cyber incident affecting the world, or a region, and customers would always come back, naturally curious to help their team figure out how these solutions could help them stay more secure. People would not only ask questions, but also bring in other departments within their companies to help showcase the value of that offering for them. This is how powerful in-product experiences can be when done right.

Freemium trials also work really well in such cases, giving customers a taste of the benefits of an add-on, upgrade or additional offering before they can buy it. Depending on the complexity of the feature of your offering, complementing your trials with some enablement increases the chances of success when it comes to converting these into a paid offering for the customer. (Adding value to everything you do is the key to growth for customers and your business)

Renewal and Advocacy

What it Means

- *To you: Retaining a customer and gaining a loyal advocate for your business, and continually putting in the work needed to maintain that advocacy.*

- *To your customers: Realizing the full value of their partnership with you, investing in their future with your business and becoming true believers in the offerings you provide.*

Okay, so renewal and advocacy are very different motions, and each deserves its own section so I have written them as entire chapters in the book (Chapters 9 and 10). But the reason I have clubbed them together in your customer-led journey is because they tie together so closely, almost as end results of all the work you put in for the other phases.

It's a natural understanding that when customers experience a smooth and frictionless journey in the other phases described above, renewals are an obvious occurrence. But it's still important to treat them as a separate motion because they do involve a bit of work (contracts, procurements cycles etc.) from both parties and ensuring a smooth process for renewals is as important as any other phase of your customers' journey.

Advocacy may or may not come as naturally as a renewal does; most of your customers might stay with you and renew but may not be raving fans or true advocates of your product. This is the key differentiator between when a customer is driven by convenience vs being true believers in your brand (and we're not aiming to achieve this for all our customers, but focusing on driving loyalty with ones that show signs of true partnership and win them as raving fans.)

A key driver for success in all phases of a customer-led journey is the consistency of information flow. Customer success is a destination and all the steps from proposal to renewal and beyond have to be collaborative for the journey to be frictionless. Now that we know what the journey looks like, let's look at how your teams can make use of the right metrics to power each stage of the journey to drive value for customers and for the business.

Chapter 5
METRICS THAT MATTER

"Not everything that can be counted counts and not everything that counts can be counted."
- Albert Einstein

If you go by the old adage "Customer is King", then the keys to that kingdom are hidden behind the right data points. Think of a company's goals for its customers; the aim is to retain them, grow them, and make them successful. How do you make that happen? You do a number of things that we have outlined in the chapters thus far, but how do you know which one of your strategies is working better than others and what improvements are being brought about by the constant innovation you put into your customer-centricity strategy? That cause and effect relationship is showcased by the data you capture.

In this chapter, we will explore the world of customer data from two angles: Metrics for customer health, and business metrics that help measure the impact of your customer-centricity strategy.

Asking the Right Questions

Before we take a deeper dive into the world of data and metrics, let's look at the fundamental questions one must ask to track the three key goals a company wants to achieve when it comes to its existing customers:

- **Increase Retention:**
  - Why do some customers leave and others stay? (aka causes of churn, turn back to the churn section in Chapter 2 to re-read some of the most common ones)
  - The value gap or unmet expectation: What did they want versus what they got?
  - How replaceable is your product or service?

- **Increase Expansion:**
  - Why do customers buy more from you?

- **Increase Advocacy:**
  - What are the common traits of customers that become raving fans versus those that just renew?
  - What causes a lack of attachment to your brand (the difference between a great experience and an average or below-average one)

The problem is that most organizations don't ask these questions in their data journey, or worse still, assume they know those answers without qualitative or quantitative information to back it up. Answering the "why" question before the "how" and "what" questions is very important when it comes to your customer data strategy. Companies collect customer data and build business metrics around it so that they can:

- Understand their customers better
- Make business decisions
- Drive experiences that matter

Renowned customer success strategist Ed Powers says that, *"When it comes to data, small changes to your strategy could be having a big impact. Research from Bessmer group shows that a 1% improvement in net retention increased enterprise value by $100M. The key challenge for companies is to separate the meaningful signals from noise, and use them to make more informed decisions. The importance of a data strategy goes beyond just looking at the numbers; it involves understanding the true nature of variance to analyze and predict churn and accurately build customer health scores. So, your customer success team should have at least one person who is well-versed with data and is dedicatedly working with other teams to map out and analyze which metrics amongst the wealth of customer data you have really matter for value and success."*

I couldn't agree more with Ed's statement because I have lived on both sides of the equation. I have worked with companies that have had health scores and metrics so powerful that it made the customer success team's job so easy just by enabling them to be proactive and focusing on the right customers at the right time. I have also seen companies where the health score existed, but it didn't capture the right data points with correct weightages and we ended up seeing a lot of customers who were "green" on our dashboards but would still be dissatisfied and would ultimately churn. The analysis revealed a gap in the health score, but the business insisted these were the right metrics (something needed to change but no one cared to figure out what it was in the midst of all the firefighting). The difference was that the company who got the health scores right had a dedicated data team measuring, analyzing and interpreting health scores.

Aside from customer health metrics, companies also have business metrics that are plastered on to management presentations and discussed to no end in leadership meetings; and that is great, because we need more discussion on customer metrics that impact business. What does not happen though, is education of what these metrics mean to the business for individual teams. If you throw the term Net Retention Rate (NRR), for example, at a marketing or product manager, chances are they're not going to be able to explain it very well. And that doesn't reflect on their lack of knowledge; it indicates the need for a company-wide enablement to help people understand metrics that help them quantify their efforts and results better. As you embark on your data journey for customer success, identifying the right data points for your customers and your business goes hand in hand with ensuring consistency and collaboration between teams and ensuring a common understanding of the business goals behind your most important data points.

360 View or 360 Value: Capturing Customer Health

A "360 view" of the customer has become quite the buzzword in the technology industry these days. Some call it a truly necessary and achievable reality, while a few experts have deemed it a myth. Let me give you my take on it.

There are no two ways about the fact that knowing your customers through data and analyzing their behaviours and health is crucial. But here's the reality - you could be using the most powerful Customer Data Platform (CDP) in the world and yet you may not achieve what you want because the basic fundamental of a CDP is that it pulls data from different sources used by you. What goes in is what comes out. And what goes in is a substantial amount of time, money and effort to streamline all your internal systems; add to these technical challenges, and the time spent by your teams in the process. All of this makes it a significant amount of work. This is an important consideration while making an investment in a customer data platform, and while some companies have taken the journey quite far along, most have to abandon it mid-way. So, what is the starting point then? My suggestion is to prioritize. Companies should prioritize customer outcomes and base their health metrics and data strategy on that rather than buzzwords (after all, isn't that what true customer-centricity is all about?)

So whether your endgame is to deploy a customer data platform and achieve a 360 customer view in the end using that, or something else, here are some foundational pillars that help you think about the different aspects of customer health data in the right way.

- **Purchase and Usage:**
    - *Who bought what*: This is basic subscription and company information such as what did a customer buy from you, what is their business, how much they spend with you, who your key users and champions are. Remember that different users within the same organization can have varied goals and success outcomes,

and understanding them is the key to their championship and advocacy.

- *How are they using it*: This comprises factors such as licence utilization, how much time do they spend on your platform, how often do they login and what parts of the product do they spend more time on. Your account-based experiences and meaningful touchpoints are fueled by this data.

- *What kind of issues do they raise*: A customer who has never logged a support ticket is either doing perfectly well or just doesn't care much about what they've bought from you. Customer success is not a support function, but the kind of support tickets your customers log give you a wealth of information about how they use your product and what areas of the product they care most about, and where they face most issues (which might give you a chance to solve their adoption challenges proactively).

- *How do they consume the resources you provide*: The way customers consume resources on your knowledge base, learning management and training content, and other resources such as blogs or whitepapers tells you what matters most to them, both within the realms of what they have purchased from you, and also your additional offerings. Adding value to your customers' journey by making use of this qualitative information and asking the right questions at the right time paves the path for a trusted partnership and a natural expansion conversation.

- **Behavioural tendencies that drive value or indicate risk:**
Studying customer behaviour and finding a baseline for commonalities and differences in tendencies that lead to opposite ends of the centricity spectrum, namely risk and value, help you add to your existing segmentation strategy. This information further feeds into account-based experiences that help predict outcomes, prevent churn and promote value as applicable.

Understanding customers' propensity towards behaviours that indicate risk also helps you prioritize risk and act early on helping customers that can still be saved. It can help you establish the relationship between your health metrics and actual churn and help you reflect on the accuracy of your risk ratings in predicting outcomes. It also feeds into your acquisition model to help your teams qualify and acquire right-fit customers.

When you look at all the data points that encompass the information above, you will be able to effectively analyze the contrast between what causes a customer to renew, what leads to churn for your product, and what behaviours drive advocacy and loyalty. Using a combination of the right customer data points to build an effective and accurate health score is the key to healthy customers for life, and helping your team focus on the right customers at the right time in their upsell, advocacy and churn-prevention efforts.

Business Metrics for Customer Success

Your business runs on numbers, and for customer-centric organizations, there is a heavy focus on numbers that tell how your business is spending and earning money through your customers. But knowing these numbers as leaders is not enough, these metrics need to be closely understood and shared as KPIs between your teams along with health and behaviour data for your customers. While there are many metrics that businesses take into account to quantify progress in their journey towards customer-centricity, I have picked a few that I think are most important (in no particular order) for a business to educate their teams on and build shared accountability into their KPIs:

- **Customer Acquisition Cost (CAC)**: We touched upon Customer Acquisition costs briefly in Chapter 2. The cost of acquiring a customer is every dollar you spend on lead generation, marketing, personnel costs etc., divided by the number of customers you acquire during a certain period. Every business exists to grow and make profit, and knowledge of your CAC in comparison to profits and lifetime value generated by your customers is an important factor to consider while making decisions about which acquisition channels are worth investing in, and which ones do not have a high yield.

- **Customer Lifetime Value (CLV)**: Customer Lifetime Value is the revenue a customer generates during the course of their journey with you. The beauty of this metric is that it looks at the average lifetime value generated by your active customers in relation to churn and expansion patterns, and can be calculated either using historical data or be built as a predictive model.

  It is a crucial metric for businesses with a subscription pricing model as it showcases when your customer relationship translates into actual profits for the business and how that profitability grows over time. A high CLV is also an indication of your product being a good market fit and the value of your efforts and investment in a customer-centricity strategy. It feeds into the effectiveness of metrics such as customer acquisition cost; by helping you understand the value customers accrue over time, acquisition costs can be adjusted and justified. Companies also often look at their CLV to CAC ratio to give them an understanding of how long it takes for a customer to turn profitable.

- **Customer Retention Cost (CRC):** Just like customer acquisition, there is a cost and effort for customer retention as well. This is quantified by your Customer Retention Cost (CRC). Your Customer Retention Cost is the sum of all your retention efforts such as employee salaries, customer marketing budget, technology investments etc., divided by the number of current active customers during a certain time period.

Measuring the financial investment required to retain customers helps leaders quantify the return on investment for your customer success program and also allows you to gauge whether your customer lifetime value justifies this investment. It helps you refocus costs on initiatives that can be digitally scaled to allow for maximum effectiveness and balance the financial investment that goes into your high touch customer success model.

- **Customer Feedback:** Customer feedback is your biggest source of truth about sentiment, loyalty and advocacy. Feedback can be collected in many forms, both qualitative and quantitative, one-to-one or one-to-many. We elaborate on the importance of customer feedback, and a strategy to collect and respond to feedback in the next chapter. It is one of the most powerful metrics for customer-centricity when implemented and used in the right way.

- **Net Retention Rate (NRR):** This metric is my personal favourite of all, and it's not without good reason.

Net Revenue Retention Rate measures the overall impact of your retention strategy by giving you a percentage rate of your total recurring revenue including expansions, downsells and churn against your total recurring revenue from existing customers during a given time. The power of this metric lies in the fact that all of the data that makes up this metric is rooted in your customers' outcomes, and is combined into one number.

Studies have established a strong correlation between the NRR of SaaS companies and their business valuation due to the sustainable, efficient revenue growth story showcased behind this metric. With the growing understanding of the power of customer success, NRR is an important metric that helps customer success leaders showcase the return on investment on the company's customer-centricity strategy.

One thing to note is that because NRR is a lagging metric, it should not be the only metric you should be using to measure the performance of your customer success teams. However, everything that feeds into the NRR i.e all the efforts that proactively go into preventing churn and downsells, encouraging upsells, and promoting value should form part of your customer success team's KPIs and those efforts will reflect in your improved net retention rate.

Data Works Best When it is Used in the Right Way

A great understanding of data comes with the responsibility of delivering actionable insights to your team and to your customers using that data.

I was once part of a business review where I saw the vendor's team present "adoption percentage" in their slides at the meeting. While the metric was presented in good faith as a potential area of improvement, no one could explain how they came up with that number and what it meant. My only thought was: Adoption is not looking great, which means the product isn't being used well, but wait, adoption is a wide term, what does it mean in this context? And it is such a dangerous thing when it is left open for interpretation. All the customer executives would think would be: I don't exactly know what this product does for us but it's certainly not doing a great job of doing what it's supposed to do for my team.

There are no points for guessing that it is exactly what happened and the meeting went downhill from there. The metrics opened a can of worms that encouraged questioning of the value of the product in a not-so-positive way.

As account teams, there is a lot of subscription, usage, pricing, adoption, and roadmap information thrown at us all the time. What needs to happen along with the delivery of that information is education on how that information is to be used (and not be used), internally and externally. Again, the point of this story is not to bash the account team who put a lot of thought and effort into preparing for this customer review, it is to highlight the need for enablement and deeper dives into what metrics mean, and how (or if) they are to be presented to customers.

A good data strategy goes beyond just collecting, reporting and showcasing metrics and statistics; it feeds back into where it comes from to make your metrics better. So, once you've answered the why, how and what questions for data, ask yourself this:

- **Benchmarking**: How can you establish benchmarks for what good, average, and bad looks like for each of these data points? And how can you improve each of these metrics?

- **Education**: How can you educate your teams to use these metrics? How do they fuel your marketing, retention, segmentation and account-based experience strategies? How are your customer success teams using this data to prioritize their engagements with customers? And most importantly, are you using this data to build a digital customer success motion that delivers outcomes for your customers at scale?

- **Predictive Analysis**: How can you use this data to predict customer behaviour based on current trends? Predictive analysis takes your data strategy to the next level by helping you forecast outcomes and next best-steps. It is something that requires some investment in Artificial Intelligence and data science but this is an investment more than worth its weight in gold. It supercharges your customer-centricity and growth, and puts your team at the forefront of customer issues to proactively reduce churn and increase customer satisfaction.

- **Continual Improvement**: As you mature in your data journey, it's always a good idea to revisit your metrics and evaluate their relevance to modify and add ones that make sense to your customers and your business. Each business runs differently and has different needs as they scale, and your customer data needs to stay relevant for it to align with your growth strategy.

Behind all of those statistics and the qualitative insights is a story, and if you can take your teams on that storytelling journey, it will lead to great outcomes for your customers and for your business.

Chapter 6
CAPTURING FEEDBACK AND CLOSING THE LOOP

"Companies that actively engage in Voice of Customer programs spend 25% less on customer retention than those that don't."

- Gartner

You're at a nice dinner at a beautiful restaurant; the ambience is perfect, the wine pairs really well with your delectable starters, and everything seems great. As you savour that first sip and bite and look up, you see the server hovering close to you with an ear-to-ear grin to ask "So, how is it?" before you have had a moment to think about it. You'll probably nod and smile, but definitely have an afterthought, *"I needed to be given a moment to swallow my food before being asked how I liked it"*. Now if this happened constantly during your meal, you would probably end your night with an average experience that could have been superior, and you would've loved to convey that to the restaurant, if the feedback was taken at the right moments. Feedback is a powerful tool when strategically placed at the right points in the customer journey.

Every company strives to do their best to attract new buyers and stay close to their existing ones. Knowing your customers' expectations from your brand, why they buy, the things they love, things that could be improved, and things that make them stay with you or leave, will help you evolve with the evolving needs of the market.

While most companies have a customer feedback and voice of customer program in place, very few are able to unlock and showcase it's full potential. Asking for feedback is crucial, so is knowing how to use that feedback and communicating back to customers how their feedback was used to drive actual change in your product or the way you service them. That's what closes the loop.

As much as listening to your customers is important, it must be done in the right way, and at the right times to yield the best results for your customers and your business.

All Customers are not Created Equal; Neither is All Kinds of Feedback

While all your customers are important to your business and deserve to be treated and satisfied to your best possible ability, not all of them hold equal strategic value for your business. Like all other things in your business, your customer segmentation strategy applies to customer feedback too. Your high-value customers hold the key to long-term profitability; that does not mean you don't listen to or care for the needs of your other customers, it simply means that the strategy for listening to the feedback of high-value customers and involving them in the way you transform your business to be more customer-centric should be different too. And in doing that, you will be able to subsequently cater to the needs of all of your other customers in a better way, leading to a win-win for everyone.

When capturing the voice of your high-value customers, your program should aim to look at the risks, opportunities and alignment elements of your high-value customer relationships, and see which parts of this feedback can be scaled into catering to the needs of your entire customer base.

While there are numerous ways to slice and dice the concept of customer feedback, keeping in mind the theme of customer-centricity and thinking like the customer, I have categorized customer feedback into two kinds:

- Methods of capturing feedback that actively involve your customers in the process and allow them to directly see the impact of the feedback for themselves and for future buyers. Your ideal audience for receiving and actively participating in this category of feedback are your high-value prospects and customers.

- Things that help your customers indirectly in the long run by helping inform you of their satisfaction and experience that feeds back into your business processes.

Let's look at the kinds of feedback for both of these categories in more detail.

Feedback mechanisms that actively involve the customer

Things that help your customers directly, i.e. they can see the direct impact of those kinds of feedback on themselves and future buyers. Some of the examples of this form of feedback include:

- **Win/Loss Analysis**
  The process of a win/loss analysis involves reaching out to customers/prospects you recently won or lost business with. These are usually done in an interview format, and best practice is to have them conducted by a trained third party who asks the right questions, and then delivers the information they retained to you for further analysis. It also makes it easier for people to share their unbiased opinion more openly if this is done by a third party.

Insights from win/loss analysis from key deals that you close or lose can be a great source of learning for your business about the market's perception of your brand and product, what makes you stand out from or lose to your competitors, and the aspects of your product or sales process that are important to your audience. Research shows that companies who incorporate win/loss analysis as part of their post-sales process have higher growth and retention than those who don't.

- **Customer Community**
  A customer community is a closed space for customers to interact with your brand and with other fellow users. The concept of communities is driven by the basic human want to network and socialize. Communities can be as simple as a social media group, or a portal that forms an extension of your product experience.

  Building a highly engaged customer community is an exciting challenge. A lot of brands create buzz and activity around their customer communities through exclusive invites, rewards for interacting within the community etc. Communities encourage interaction between customers through sharing of answers to questions, best practices, pros and cons of your products, and other shared experiences. Communities are a great way to pick up on customer feedback and interact with your customers; in fact, they could form the biggest source of product feature suggestions for you. Customers who post great things about you and are power users who help others by answering their questions could be great candidates for a case study or interview. Similarly, people who have shared negative feedback can be contacted for further assistance and to understand how you can help them. Either way, they form a great source of interaction and learning.

Open communities that are not limited to existing customers can be a great source of information for your potential buyers too. Disney has an online community called planDisney (earlier known as Walt Disney World Moms Panel), that allows a select group of special panellists who are experienced Disney World visitors to answer questions for people planning a Disney vacation. It fosters trust by helping people get advice from real "champions" and experienced customers of the brand and aids their decision making process.

- **Customer Advisory Boards**
  Your strategic customers are more than champions and advocates, they are influencers of your product and company direction, and that is exactly what customer advisory boards are all about. A customer advisory board comprises a select group of customers who meet at regular intervals to lend their insights to your product roadmap, with early testing, ideas, etc. Members of this group are generally chosen from your highest-value customer segment, and are industry thought leaders and market experts in addition to being your most valuable users. Customer advisory boards encourage open dialogue in a controlled environment, the agenda of which is governed by a well-articulated charter (if you're starting to play with the idea of having a customer advisory board, a clear charter outlining goals and objectives for the group as well as the agenda and themes helps keep the discussion relevant and fruitful for everyone involved). Customers that are part of this group can also become early testers of new feature releases, and most importantly still remain torch-bearers for your brand as they move roles and go to other organizations.

Advisory board discussions are themed around topics such as:

- Validating the direction of your product
- Industry trends and their impact on your product and unique value proposition
- New opportunities, capabilities and market segments that shape your future strategy for growth and expansion.

- **Customer Interviews and Focus Groups**
Customer interviews are a great way to gauge in-depth sentiment after an event or a milestone in your customer's journey. These can be used in conjunction with surveys to uncover needs and perceptions, understand the customer's viewpoint better, and to build connections and richer personas. Interviews are a great follow up tool after events such as onboarding, renewal, or after a customer answers a survey to capture their thoughts and areas for improvement, to win their trust and championship and deepen the relationship further.

Focus groups are also a uniquely powerful way to receive deep, nuanced insights from your users. A great example of focus groups is interviewing a group of users from the same persona but different organizations to understand the commonalities and differences in their goals and expectations of your product. Focus groups can be led by an external consultant or by your own customer success or marketing team, as long as the person conducting the group has a very clear idea of what they want to achieve out of the session and how they will do it. Leading focus groups requires strong interpersonal and leadership skills.

Feedback mechanisms that help your customers by helping you improve your business processes

Some forms of feedback help your customers indirectly in the long run by improving the way you do things, and subsequently enhancing your customer experience. Your customers may not feel like they are an active part of the change undertaken as a result of this category of feedback, but they feel the improvements made as a result of it. A few examples of these are:

- **Net Promoter Score (NPS)**
  Net Promoter Score or NPS is a metric that measures customer loyalty by asking one simple question: *"On a Scale of 0 to 10, how likely are you to recommend a product or service to a friend?"* It may or may not be accompanied by an open text question that allows the receiver of the survey to explain why they gave a particular rating. This

question enables you to discover the main drivers that differentiate promoters from detractors and passive respondents. You can also ask what you can do to improve their experience.

Respondents who give you a high score of 9 or 10 are *promoters* (your loyal and enthusiastic customers), those who score you 7 or 8 are *passives* (satisfied but not enough to be loyal advocates), and the ones who rate you 6 or below are *detractors* (people with a below-par experience with your product). Your NPS score is the percentage of detractors subtracted from the percentage of promoters.

There has recently been a lot of healthy debate in the customer success world about the relevance of NPS as a metric. I think like everything else, it's how you use this metric that defines its relevance and effectiveness for your business. For example, for individual customers, if you send NPS surveys to executive buyers (financial decision makers who pay for your product), and marry that data with in-product feedback from daily users of the same customer company, it forms a powerful indicator of their renewal health. You can also layer your NPS with churn data to link it to renewal prediction analytics in general. Some companies segment their NPS to decipher patterns in certain kinds of buyer behaviour and act on improving areas where detractor scores are in highest numbers.

The more data you put alongside your NPS, the more powerful your understanding of the why of this metric becomes for your business.

- **Customer Effort Score (CES)**
  Problems are inevitable in the real world. What matters is how efficiently you solve the smallest and biggest problems for your customers. This ranges from how easy it is to find simple information on your website to the time it takes for a customer to chase down the right team to talk to about an issue. That's what your customer effort score (CES) denotes. Helping improve serviceability for your customers across different channels and in their human interactions with you to make things simple and easy to find is the key to improving your customer effort score.

CES is an important metric to measure satisfaction and loyalty, and is also relatively easy to implement across multiple feedback channels. It feeds into your customer support and marketing strategy and helps optimize the way information is presented and delivered to customers through these teams. It is important to note, however, that the true power of CES is unleashed when it is used along with other customer satisfaction metrics such as Customer Satisfaction and Net Promoter Score (NPS) to get a fuller, more accurate picture of the customer's experience.

- **Customer Satisfaction Score (CSAT)**
  CSAT scores measure the overall satisfaction levels with your product or service, or a milestone in the customer's journey. It is meant to get an "in the moment" reaction after an event or milestone, which is different from NPS that measures the ongoing, overall satisfaction with your product or service.

  CSAT surveys can be tailored and used at different points in the customer journey that define "memorable moments" or milestones to gauge not only their experience but also the expected next steps and action items. A lot of companies complement their customer onboarding program with an onboarding CSAT survey sent after the completion of the onboarding to ensure it was a satisfactory experience for all involved and to ensure they have everything they need to get started on the right foot with your product. Companies also do pre and post-renewal surveys to gauge customers' sentiment about the renewal process, or after a support ticket has been closed. You can really use CSAT surveys at any point in the customer journey as long as they pose meaningful questions for the right audience and are complemented with a follow up conversation that closes the loop and makes the customer feel at ease.

Like any other metric, CSAT scores should be supplemented with follow up and further information to get an idea of the key drivers behind the rating which can be used for continual improvement.

Make Feedback Work for You

Like any other data containing qualitative and quantitative metrics, a Voice of Customer program can very quickly spiral out of control if the feedback you receive is not categorized and channelled in the right way. It's crucial to help your team separate signals from noise to help use the feedback to solve key customer problems, understand what is working and be proactive for your customers and for your business. Let's look at some of the best practices for an effective Voice of Customer program:

- **Know your why**
  For each method of customer feedback you implement, define a clear purpose. Having customers fill out a bunch of surveys or sit through a bunch of interviews not clearly knowing what value "they" receive out of it may deter participation and response rates. Not knowing the goal can lead to wasted time for the customer and may deter them from participating in future feedback opportunities, and a lack of clearly defined questions can lead to vague answers or worse, could lead you on a path to making product updates that are not relevant or are likely to move the value needle negatively.

  As with any other customer interaction, preparation is key to fruitful execution, and that starts with having a well-defined outcome that drives your method. Ask the right audience the right questions and get the right responses that help you help your customers.

- **Keep it simple**
  Simplicity in the delivery of your Voice of Customer program is key to its efficacy. Overcomplicating the questions in a survey or in an interview can confuse the messaging and hence the response. This is not to say don't ask

follow up questions or collect qualitative data; just make it relevant to the feedback mechanism you're deploying.

The simplicity aspect also applies to how you deliver customer feedback data to your internal teams for insight and action because that is what drives real growth and change. Categorize your customer feedback in a way that makes most sense for your business, and make it available to your team in a centralized location such as your internal CRM system or any other platform that you use to help them identify recurring themes in the different aspects of feedback from the same customer.

- **Use the feedback to initiate a deeper conversation**
  Companies who actively reach out to customers to discuss their feedback, whether it's positive or negative, are considered more trustworthy than those that don't. Always remember that feedback is a means to an end, which is to initiate continual improvement in your business and products by taking into account the things that matter to your customers. Closing the loop enhances trust and deepens your relationship with your customers. It also encourages your customers to share their thoughts more openly with you because

they know what they say matters and that your business cares about what they think.

- **Communicate that you have listened to your customers**

  I cannot stress enough on the value of taking some time to reach out to your customers to thank them for their feedback and to let them know you've listened and made changes or improved. This can be done via one-on-one communication or at scale, depending on what feedback was collected and how it is relevant to a particular customer or a group of customers. For example, group communication from your leadership team to all or some of your customers with a "you asked, we listened" message works really well and goes a long way in establishing trust and loyalty for your business.

I talked to Laura Beavin-Yates, Senior Vice President for Customer Success at Immersion Neuroscience. Laura drove a 46% improvement in user adoption for customers who were in their first month of implementation by making simple, effective tweaks to their onboarding process driven by customer feedback. The team at Immersion learned that new users were feeling overwhelmed by having to choose different options in the tool and weren't getting to value after signing up for a trial because they couldn't decide where to use the software first. Laura's team used this feedback and other usage data to implement a new product-led onboarding process, which presents a small set of measurement options during onboarding. Now, after the user makes a measurement selection from a small set of options, they are automatically provided results and insights, which has driven faster time to first value.

Laura says, *"Customer feedback is a vital catalyst for product improvements and we put it at the heart of our business because we know we're nothing without our customers - but also because we're dedicated to helping our customers capture and implement their own customer feedback! All businesses should prioritize customer feedback. Operating without it is like flying a plane without a radar system – you're basically flying blind. One of the key responsibilities of our Customer Success team at Immersion is educating customers on the importance of gathering feedback.*

Customer feedback is one of the most powerful compasses you can use to guide an outcome-focused journey – not only for your own company but also for the customers you serve. When possible, I encourage and recommend embracing unique approaches that allow you to capture genuine, unbiased feedback."

Good, bad, ugly - all kinds of customer feedback is beautiful. The real value of feedback comes out when it is married to the goals and outcomes you'd like to achieve for your business and your customers, and the output is used to make informed business decisions and have memorable customer conversations that build trust, increase value and strengthen partnerships.

Chapter 7
STRUCTURING WINNING CONVERSATIONS

If you ask seasoned sales and customer success professionals the secret to keeping customers engaged, they will tell you it is to become their "trusted advisor". And when you witness these stalwarts having meaningful conversations and creating raving fans using the power of trust-based relationships, they make it all look like a cakewalk. What you do not see is the hard work and continual effort that goes on behind the scenes into achieving that trusted advisor status, because I can promise you, customers do not hand that title out as easily as one would imagine. So, for every meaningful talk track that is used in a customer meeting which sweeps them off their feet and paves the path to a valuable conversation, there is a massive amount of preparation and research in the background.

Having conversations that build value continually and discuss things that truly matter to your customers is the key to establishing and maintaining trust. Now, if you're a business leader or someone in a customer-facing role, chances are that you are a great communicator already, So, the aim of this chapter is not to teach you the art of conversation. What we will do is unpack the science behind effectively aligning with your high value customers to create wins for them, your company and for your own self and how you can leverage your conversational skills to steer discussions that matter.

High-Value Customers: Great Expectations, Greater Results

One of the core concepts of customer-centricity is to align the long-term profitability of your business to the needs and outcomes of your most valuable customers. Let's unpack the 'high-value customer' part of this definition a bit further.

I've mentioned in earlier chapters that *"not all customers are created equal"* - Your high value customers are your biggest source of learning and profit, and hence need to be handled strategically. This customer segment doesn't just include customers with the highest spend; there could be customers in this category that may not be high-revenue at the time, but have high expansion potential, and hold the key to things such as industry reputation, thought leadership, innovation and expansion potential, which makes them a gold mine of learning and eventually, profitability for your business.

Your high value customers are loyal advocates that are fully connected to your brand value, become great references and promote your brand through word of mouth marketing, and they also make up for a sizeable portion of your company's revenue. Naturally, with the colossal value these customers bring to the table, they have high expectations of your team in the way they are serviced and delivered success to.

The power of all of the strategies and methods we have discussed in this book so far, right from taking the first steps towards customer-centricity, aligning your teams, collecting data and feedback contributes to how you align with and deliver value to your most important customers using a highly personalized customer success program. This is also commonly known in the industry as *high-touch customer success.*

A high-touch customer success model for your customers is a worthy investment, not only because it helps you retain and grow your high value clients, but also because your high-touch customer success strategy feeds into the success of your entire customer base, and helps you tailor your marketing communications, customer acquisition and digital customer success programs.

Your customer segmentation strategy helps you narrow down who the high value customers of your business are by helping you narrow down the criteria you use to define "high-value". This could be current recurring revenue, future spend potential, industry reputation etc. (We discussed the importance of account segmentation in Chapter 4 under Value Realization). Once you know who these customers are, the next step is to define a strategy for engaging with them in the most effective way. Naturally, this will call for several human touchpoints and ongoing conversations that help define and deliver the value and outcomes that matter to these customers.

Let's look at the essential components of a high-touch customer success program:

- **Documentation**
  As someone who has a lot of ideas and thoughts, I have a personal belief - if you can't write it down and explain it to someone, it's not a good plan. And I follow this rule in my professional and personal life. Planning success with and for your strategic customers is more than having an idea in your head about how your engagements will go. Every step of this journey requires you to document a plan and share it with your customer and internal teams so that everyone is on the same page, and understands their role in contributing to the success of the relationship. Customer planning documentation varies according to the needs of your business and your customers, but two of the must-haves for me in my customer success

arsenal are account plans and success plans (yes, these are different from one another and each has their own purpose and value):

Account Plans: When you sell your product or service to a high value account, your vision of what you want to achieve out of that customer relationship doesn't end with the sale. As you go through the sales process, your sales teams discover the key needs and success criteria of these customers, the risks associated with delivering the vision you promised them, the opportunity for further growth and the steps needed to bring your vision of the future relationship with these customers to life. All of this information is what your account dreams aka account plans are made of.

This is your team's plan on a page, containing everything you need in order to achieve the internal goal of growth and retention with your key accounts. It contains what I like to call the "dirty details" that help your team paint a picture of what needs to be done to help the customer see value in everything you do with them, and any potential roadblocks that they need to be aware of?

Who creates account plans?

Sales teams start the first draft of an account plan with everything they uncover in the sales cycle; things like which stakeholder isn't leaning in favour of your product as much as the others, which competitors were in the mix (and if we have any wallet share with our competitors on the account. Yes, this happens a lot more than we can imagine. Big enterprises use multiple vendors simultaneously for the same purpose), how we manage different stakeholders, what is the vision and the next steps to not only renew but also upsell and grow the account.

This information can be used as the "currency" to transfer the account into the hands of your account management and customer success teams, who will then take the responsibility of updating and maintaining the account plan, and bringing the vision to life. Account plans, when done right, are the "perfect handover" from pre-sales to customer success teams and are extremely helpful in ensuring the long term success of your team.

Naturally, account plans are for internal use only, and can be done on a simple one page template in a spreadsheet or document, or using software that then makes use of the insights in the plan to feed into your marketing, customer success and executive engagement strategy for that customer.

- *Success Plans*: Delivering success to your customers by helping them achieve their goals and outcomes is not the sole responsibility of your team as a vendor. It is a collaborative effort that involves the customer as well. Success plans outline the steps in that joint effort and help assign timelines and accountabilities for tasks that form part of the customer's outcomes.

Who creates Success Plans?
Success plans are created by the customer success team in close collaboration with key champions and stakeholders at the customers' end. Usually, a first draft based on the team's understanding of the goals and outcomes of the customer (which comes from your account plan), acts as a great start for a discussion with the customer to develop a definition of what success looks like for them and what are the steps needed to get there. This can then be broken down into individual tasks

and activities with timelines and most importantly, milestones that signify different steps in the achievement of those goals.

As the goals and priorities of the customer evolve with time, the information in the success plan is updated to reflect that and reviewed regularly between the customer and yourself.

Customer success plans are an amazing tool to showcase your commitment to delivering value and also highlighting key milestones and aha moments in the customers journey. And by making the customer accountable for their parts in this journey, you help them stay on track and ensure they assign time to do what's needed from their end to achieve their desired outcome.

- **Stakeholder mapping and executive sponsorship** When managing high value customer relationships, there are often multiple stakeholders involved at both ends. Having a clear understanding of who is involved and what conversations are happening at each level is very important to ensure consistency in the messaging and an understanding of goals and objectives. Stakeholder mapping helps ensure different members of your team are engaging with the right stakeholders at the customer's end to understand their different perspectives, influences and motivations.

Your day-to-day customer contacts may be seeing success in the use of your product, but they may not always be privy to other initiatives at their company that you can be a part of. That's where the value of executive engagement comes in. Having multiple people at different levels engaged with different customer stakeholders can help you make sure that your relationship is not being gatekept by a single person or only a certain group with a limited set of objectives. An important thing to be mindful of here is to make sure that the flow of internal communications between the different groups/ individuals managing customer stakeholders is maintained. This ensures consistency in the messaging to customers and helps your team in being proactive and better prepared for their conversations.

- **Touchpoints for strategic alignment** Your high-value customers expect you to be on the same page with them about their needs and outcomes. Regular touchpoints with them pave the way for a continued conversation on how you can collectively work to achieve those goals. While these touchpoints cover everything from online and in-person meetings to emails, webinars, feedback surveys and any other means of reaching out to the customer, I've listed below the three main types of touchpoints that help keep relevant conversations going in a high-touch customer success program:

- *Onboarding sessions*: Onboarding is more than training. An onboarding program is not only your chance to show your customers' users how your product works, but also how it works for them. A great onboarding program caters to the varied needs of different kinds of users and also acts as a point of validating the goals set out by the customer during the buying cycle.

  Make this touchpoint really engaging for your users and you will take the first step towards a trusted relationship.

  High-touch onboarding programs are the right mix of metrics, strategy, processes and flexibility to help your team and your customers make the most out of them. Equip your team with playbooks, checklists and templates to help them onboard different user personas but also teach them how to tailor the program as and when the customer's situation calls for it.

Your onboarding sessions are also a great time to validate the goals in your success plans with your champions and lay out the program of work needed to achieve these goals. This is a document you can carry into the rest of the customer's journey with you to showcase the progress you're making together.

- *Recurring value sessions:* Once the customer is past the onboarding phase of their journey and work towards realizing the value of your product in their day-to-day work life, setting up some time to regularly review progress with them is really important. The frequency of these meetings depends on what works for you and the customer.

Remember, these are more than just "check-ins". They give you a chance to ensure that your product and it's value stays front of mind for your most valuable customers and it doesn't get lost in the midst of other priorities. For these sessions to yield maximum value for both parties, they have to be the right mix of showcasing progress, determining next steps and agreeing on a plan of action before you meet next. There will be times when your customer will be busy with other things and it is important to be mindful of not being overly pushy with what they have to do next. In these cases, be sure to offer help, show flexibility and empathy, but also document any delays to ensure nothing falls through the cracks.

- **Business Objectives Review:** These are also commonly known as Executive Business Reviews (EBRs) or Quarterly Business Reviews (QBRs). When done right, business reviews complement the touchpoints you have with daily users and champions by showcasing progress, reinstating value and building trust with executive stakeholders on the customer's side.

My top tip for getting these right is to prepare for these meetings "with the customer". Yes, you read that right. If you set a goal with the daily users and champions of your product to help make them look good in front of their leaders in these business reviews, they will work with you to ensure that these touchpoints are a success.

Business reviews really need to pack a punch. The worst thing is to make the customer executives sit through a long meeting, overload them with information and have them walk away with few or no takeaways. This goes beyond just presenting a slide deck for the entirety of the meeting. Share an agenda and the presentation (if you're using one) well before the meeting to give everyone time to understand and contribute to the agenda. These sessions are not just a review of what has happened so far; they're also a chance to engage in a conversation about the future, so make sure you give your customer's executive team ample time to share their thoughts, ideas and future strategy.

The Trusted Advisor

Your interactions with your high-value customers are driven by strategy and fueled by the conversations your teams have with them. These conversations form the foundations of trust in your relationship with your customers, which is the key to strong, lasting relationships.

"True trust is hard to earn, easy to break and harder to rebuild" - That is the first thing one needs to know before embarking on their journey to winning

customers' trust as an individual in the customer-facing role, a leader, or as a business. There is no set playbook, strategy or process one can follow to build trust; it is the cumulative result of credibility built through small, genuine, continual actions in personal and business relationships alike.

So how do you have conversations that build and grow trust with customers? And what sets regular conversations apart from great ones? To answer that question, let's unpack the components of a business conversation:

- **Purpose**: Every conversation has a purpose. For business conversations, irrespective of whether they are held virtually or in-person, outlining the purpose and agenda of the conversation is the responsibility of the person organizing the conversation. If the conversation is organized by your customer, make sure you understand what they're looking for and prepare in advance as needed.

- **Outcomes**: All parties involved in a conversation have an outcome in mind. In customer interactions, understanding and aligning with your outcomes is crucial to the success of your conversation. This goes beyond scratching the surface or understanding immediate requirements to really understanding the "intent" or "motivation" behind the outcomes a customer wants to achieve.

- **Exchange of information:** The information exchanged during a conversation links the purpose of the conversation to the outcomes. When talking to customers, discovery through natural curiosity, and using the right data and feedback to steer conversations goes a long way in helping uncover information that will be useful in driving the relationship forward.

- **Emotions:** We do a great job of keeping our emotions aside in the business world, yet they are a key driving factor behind our decisions. It is relatively easier to gauge emotions during key moments that define happiness or frustration for a customer, but most of our interactions with customers are not defined by those moments.

The emotions during the course of the conversation are driven by the purpose of the conversation and the exchange of information. The quality of your exchange can be the difference between *"Why am I being given too much information? I will forget all about this as soon as the meeting ends!"* to *" This is useful for me. I will take note of this information and I see value in this exchange"*

- **Follow up**: Even though a follow up is not part of the conversation itself, it is an important step in continuing the connection established in the conversation, determining next steps and timelines, and ensuring all parties follow through on the agreed path forward.

What sets a regular conversation apart from a "great" one is a fine balance of the components above coupled with emotional intelligence that enables you to read your audience, listen to their needs and give them meaningful insights that matter.

Tips for Engagements that Drive Value

Like I said earlier, there is no secret recipe to building trust and becoming a trusted advisor. It is the result of a continual effort that goes into understanding your customers to a point where you can anticipate their needs and offer suggestions that help them win. I've listed below some of the tips that have helped me have effective conversations with customers in my career so far:

- *Don't try to think like the customer:*
  This seems counterintuitive but when you try and

put yourself in the customer's shoes, there is a chance you are making a lot of assumptions that may or may not be true. This can alter the way you see things. Instead, talk to your customers, they will open up and share their challenges, what matters to them and what's on their mind.

- **Plan and prepare**: Mark Twain said *"It usually takes me more than three weeks to prepare a good impromptu speech."* I'm not using this quote to indicate that all your customer conversations have to be harmonized like a symphony, but planning and preparation goes a long way in making the conversation smoother, shorter and more meaningful. You wouldn't want to spend 5 minutes in a meeting searching through your computer for a document or notes you may need, so having a clear agenda and keeping some information in your back pocket is always useful even if you don't end up using it.

- **Speak with intention, listen with attention**: I heard this quote from a friend and thought it perfectly fits into the world of customer success. Customer facing teams have so much information on hand about the customer, their health, the product, the roadmap, exciting upcoming stuff about your company and so much more. Holding back and realizing it may not be the right time to convey a certain piece of information to a customer is as important as knowing what information to give them at a certain point in time.

- **Set realistic expectations and follow through:** This one is kind of obvious, isn't it? Underpromise and over-deliver; never the other way round. Understand, confirm, then commit, and make sure you follow through.

- ***Your internal stakeholders are as important as your external ones:***
Customer facing teams get a lot of their information from teams that may not be customer facing. And that makes it very important for all teams to be on the same page about the information that is being conveyed to the customer. Internal stakeholder management is as important as managing your customers. For example, you wouldn't want to commit to a deadline for a project delivery that is reliant upon your technology team without consulting them first. Similarly, you wouldn't want your CEO or CCO walking into a customer meeting without full information about what's going on with that customer. That's where the magic of account and success plan documentation and internal account reviews comes in.

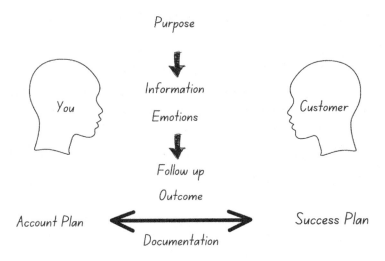

Purpose

Information

You

Emotions

Customer

Follow up

Outcome

Account Plan

Documentation

Success Plan

Great Conversations, Greater Results

Again, it's not about following these tips to guarantee successful conversations, it's about having the right mindset to prepare, listen and connect. Showing that you put your customers at the heart of your operations, and displaying an intention to partner with them and help them win in every interaction you have with them, is a skill that goes beyond the value of the product or solution you've sold to them.

Remember that people buy from people. Technology just helps accelerate the pace of achieving business goals; it is the human connection that drives success by helping people make the best use of the products and services they buy and creates mutual wins.

So, when you walk into your next customer meeting, remember that the magic lies in the *mindset!*

Chapter 8
DELIVERING VALUE AT SCALE

I love automation! It is such an amazing and powerful way to save time, increase efficiency and help people focus on things that need their attention by taking a few repeatable tasks off their hands. And being the forward-thinkers that they are, SaaS companies across the world have leveraged the power of automation to scale touchpoints with their customers. The tech-touch motion, also popularly known as digital customer success, is a game changer for companies looking to scale their customer success program.This strategy makes use of automated touchpoints via digital channels to deliver success outcomes to customers.

I love automation! (*not a typo, I said it again because I really do love it*) But, like most of us, I'm also very frustrated with unwanted emails, webinar invites, SMSes, and other forms of digital outreach coming my way, even from brands I love and constantly buy from. Because all of them are generalized, they mostly don't speak to what's important to me. If your digital customer success strategy means sending a flurry of emails with generic information after someone signs up and pays for your product, it is highly likely that you are clogging your customers' inboxes with irrelevant information. They are more likely to ignore all of it, which means even if you send them something relevant, they might miss it because they simply wouldn't care to read it.

I recently joined a popular online forum for professionals. Within the first couple of days of joining, I received an email that looked like it came from the founder of the community, asking me what are the main goals that I'd like to achieve from my membership. It was a great email and though I knew the founder didn't write it on their own, it was a great example of a digital touchpoint and I was quite impressed. Given the intent if the email was to hear from me, I responded and sent them a couple of things I'd like to achieve from my time and interactions in the forum. Guess what happened next - *nothing*! And I don't mean anything as I didn't hear back, I did. But it was not in response to my email to say my goals had been acknowledged or even something relevant to the things I had stated in regards to my goals. It was just another generic email that was probably "email number 2" sent out to a new user. What followed was exactly what you'd imagine, a series of templated updates, none of which really spoke to me as a member of that community. Disappointing right? It made me wonder, would I have had lower expectations if I hadn't been asked what I wanted to achieve and still have received a generic mix of relevant and irrelevant content?

This is the perfect example of the right intentions turned into undesirable results for your brand image because the implementation of the idea did not take the customer's needs and the importance of closing the feedback loop into account.

So, the biggest question isn't where you need a digital customer success motion? The answer to that is yes, definitely! The big question is how do you scale your customer success program in a way that keeps the basic intent of customer success alive, which is to retain and grow your customers by delivering value and helping them achieve their outcomes? And most importantly, how do you scale trust and operationalize the empathy displayed during human interactions in the digital world?

A good first step is to start simple. Like every other process or strategy you build, there is a maturity curve to digital or low-touch / no-touch models for customer success too. Instead of trying to automate everything, start with a few repeatable tasks that can be digitized. A lot of things you have done in your customer success strategy so far will help you in taking the next steps in the digitization of your customer success program. These are:

- **Your Customer Journey**: A good digital strategy for customer success begins with your *users*. A digitally-led model for customer success should focus on the journey of the end users and how you can guide them towards their outcomes using meaningful content. From a self-serve onboarding to continual self-serve touchpoints, and even automated renewals (we'll talk more about these in the next chapter), look at parts of your user journey that can be digitized.

- **Customer Data:** Your customer data makes your strategy for digital customer success smarter and more meaningful. Sending communications to a customer after certain moments that define activity or inactivity can trigger meaningful action on the customer's end. For example, you can send an email helping the customer with some self-serve material with next steps once they complete their product setup successfully. On the other hand, if a certain period of time has passed and the customer still hasn't completed their setup, you could send communication offering resources and even manual help from your team if they need it.

- **Account Segmentation:** Your account segmentation strategy can become a great feed into your digital customer success program. As your customer base grows, the volume of their activities, goals and outcomes become larger. Handling such a large volume of behaviour patterns can be quite challenging, and that's where your segmentation strategy comes into play. You can group customers according to commonalities in their sentiments, goals, outcomes, interests etc., and tailor communications you send to them based on the segments they belong to. It makes sending relevant content at scale so much easier.

The above points make it really clear that your high-touch strategy has a great role to play in your low-touch / no-touch strategy for customer success. It also indicates that your digital customer success program is not just for customers in the mid or low-tier revenue segments. When done right, this program can serve your strategic and high-value accounts equally well.

The HEART of Digital Customer Success

There are several low touch or no touch ways to execute your digital customer success strategy, ranging from but not limited to emails, webinars, ask-me-anything sessions, customer summits, customer communities, social media etc. Irrespective of the medium of delivery, the same core components that make your high touch customer success program a success are also the heart of your digital customer strategy. HEART is an acronym for Humanize, Empathize, Align, Respond and Track. Let's look at this in more detail:

- *Humanize:* Humanizing your digital-led customer success program is a crucial step. People can often tell if a communication sent to them is coming from a real human being or an automated process. They are also more likely to respond if they think it's coming from an actual person. Think of the welcome email I mentioned in the example I stated earlier in the chapter, asking about my goals. It looked like it came from the founder's email address, urging the addressee to respond and asking very clear questions about their goals. That's how you want your digital communications to look like (it was the only great part of my experience in that whole scenario!). Stop using no-reply or generic email addresses when corresponding with your customers. Sending emails from addresses that customers can respond to by simply replying to the email sent to them are much more seamless than no-reply addresses that redirect customers to look elsewhere for help if they need it.

Secondly, never lose the human touch. Letting your customers know that they can contact one of your actual team members if they need to speak with a human being is very reassuring and encourages two-way communication. The digital world can often be a lonely one, despite the vast majority of information available and a bit of a human touch when it's needed can make all the difference.

- *Empathize:* Empathy is a huge buzzword in the customer success industry, and while most organizations promise empathy, very few are actually able to live up to the hype.

So, how do we make our digital touchpoints empathetic? It starts with the little details such as simplicity in delivery, ease of use in your resources and staying in context when it comes to your customers' needs. Keeping these things in mind will enable you to tailor your touchpoints in a way that customers feel like they're receiving value in a timely manner, make it clear and easy for them to understand how they can make your product work for them, and they walk out of that experience (whether its an email, a webinar or a help page on your website) feeling like it was a good use of their time.

Your digital content can help nurture positive emotions if it is clear, easily accessible and well-aligned with what customers need.

- *Align*: Alignment is important both internally and externally. Internal alignment is necessary to keep track of the outreach to your customers via different channels and from different teams to ensure they're not receiving duplicate information or similar instances of messaging through different methods (it's the quickest way to endup in your customers' spam folder).

When it comes to aligning with customers, the series of conversations created through your digital touchpoints should speak to their needs and outcomes. Again, it goes back to understanding your customers well and ensuring relevance in your communication strategy.

- *Respond*: If your digital touchpoints ask your customers a question, or for feedback, please don't let them feel that it goes into a blackhole (if you go back to the example I gave about my experience with that online forum, that's exactly what I felt like and it's not the best experience as you can probably tell). You wouldn't leave your customers hanging if they opened a support ticket, gave you a phone call or had a conversation with you in person. Your digital strategy needs to replicate that behaviour. Opening up the channel for two-way communication and responding to your customers is a great way to scale trust.

- *Track*: You know your customer's goals, you've sent them resources and information that you think will help them achieve their desired outcomes. But do you have a way to track if they actually did? You can rely on your customer health and usage data to predict the answer to this question, or, better still, you can ask the customer. Use feedback mechanisms to track whether they were able to accomplish what they wanted to using your product and how your digital touchpoints played a role in that journey, and how you can improve. If you're using self-serve materials, be sure to track which ones are being used by customers. Closing the loop and showing that you care about your customer's results even when it's through a scaled program shows your customers that they matter to you.

The insights and analytics that come from tracking your customers' interactions with your digital touchpoints are a gold mine of information for continually improving your overall program.

Scaling Personalized Experiences

The best digital strategies for customer success do not sound or look or feel like they're digital, that is the model you should be working towards, and the key to doing this lies in personalization.

Personalization in your digital communications is so much more than just generic email templates that use your customers' names in the opening statement. Effective personalization really speaks to the customer and also gives them appropriate and intelligent responses based on their needs, input and feedback.

I talked to Dickey Singh, who is the founder and CEO of cast.app. What Dickey has built is a truly next generation system that allows for the human touch to stay alive in your digital customer success program. I asked Dickey about the importance of personalization and how we can effectively build personalization at scale for a successful digital customer success program. Here's what he said:

> "*Personalization makes your content relevant for your customers, driving engagement, and in turn, product adoption, user advocacy, customer success, and revenue growth. In a high-touch program, customer success groups can easily personalize communications and maintain intimate relationships with the small fraction of customers*

they provide services to. However, the challenge that faces most companies is that this white-glove service cannot be replicated across their entire customer base without significant investment in human resources, and that is not a scalable strategy. The solution to this lies in automation and personalization.

Effective personalization means going beyond the standard, "Hello {User's Name}". It takes into account the role of the user, where they are at in their journey with you, and the relevance of the content in their daily lives. By personalizing both the value attained and recommendation for each user at every account, you increase stickiness, leading to lower churn, higher adoption, and an unparalleled customer ROI.

For example, automate showing the ROI, SLAs, and value statement to senior executives; sharing product, support, and usage analytics with the operator; and conveying specific campaign details with the individual contributor at the customers' end. Similarly, if you send a renewal, upsell or cross-sell survey to an individual user, it's irrelevant because they may not be able to make that decision.

The medium and language of communication also plays a huge role in the effectiveness of the message. Engaging mediums play an essential role. With visual and auditory senses stimulated, such dual-modality personalized communications can be upto 6.5 times more effective. Studies have shown personalizing content and recommendations in the native language of the user also drives higher calls to action. When connecting with daily users, an in-product recommendation or messaging may work well, but when reaching out to executives who may not use your product but are responsible for financial decisions relating to it, an email is a more effective method of outreach.

Lastly, remember that less is more. Reduce the quantity of content and recommendations made but do an excellent job of explaining it. The best time to drive product adoption, ask for feedback, or drive a sales action, is right after a convincing personalized explanation."

Customer Marketing: The Heartbeat of Your Digital Customer Success Program

Working on an effective digitally-led customer success program is a significant boost for your business because it allows you to touch all of your customers, no matter how big or small they are. But it is also something that requires a significant amount of effort before you start seeing results. So, the natural question is how do you do this? Which team executes this strategy?

The answer lies in a function that combines the best of the worlds of marketing and customer success, and that's how the customer marketing function was born. Customer marketing is a function that reports into your chief customer officer or head of customer success (people's opinions on where the customer marketing function sits vary, but to me it is a core part of the customer success organization). The aim of this function, which can start as one individual with a marketing background and a great understanding of customer success, and then grow into a team as you scale, is to execute your digital customer success strategy and deliver "account-based experiences" with a view to increase loyalty and championship.

Using marketing expertise to nurture existing customers drives value and helps create meaningful experiences for all user roles,which in turn positively impacts your customer lifetime value. A lot of businesses see churn in their small to medium tier customer base due to the lack of touchpoints. This segment of customers is often left out in the search for champions and advocates, when a lot of your loyal customers who are more than ready to give you raving reviews can be found here.

Dickey Singh added his thoughts on Customer Marketing. *"Companies should understand how Customer Marketing is different from acquisition marketing. While marketing to potential buyers, we make guesses about their preferences and rely on frequent A|B testing to find a message for your brand that resonates with them. In Customer Marketing, we have all the data to rely on — stakeholder usage and profile, account information, licenses, customer journey stage, segments, and more — and the task becomes summarizing and sharing the most relevant content and recommendations."*

If your SaaS business does not have a dedicated resource (or pool of resources, depending on your needs) for customer marketing, this is a sign to start thinking about it. By combining the ninja skills of a great customer success manager (read value-delivery, retention and expansion strategy) with the creative mind of a marketer, this is a complete powerhouse of a function for your business. Your customer marketing function not only helps you execute a low-touch / no touch customer success program, they also add value to it by taking charge of your customer feedback strategy, and advocacy initiatives such as webinars, customer communities, interviews and case studies etc. These initiatives drive the creation of a vibrant community of customer champions and evangelists around your offering.

Human-led Automation

The intelligence in automation and artificial intelligence comes from humans who create these programs. As such, your digital programs continually improve by learning from human interactions. Even when you're leading with digital touchpoints, make sure you make it easy for your customers to contact a human when they need to. This is a key part of making the digital-first experience seamless for your customer base. These simple options instil positive emotions and behaviours in your customers, even when they're not always talking to you in person.

You will also always have customers in every segment that are unresponsive to any form of outreach, but that doesn't mean they need you any less. I had one such customer who hadn't responded to any emails, marketing outreach, webinar invites, survey and feedback requests in months. Their usage stats showed that they were logging in and using our platform (less than regularly, but this was the only sign of a heartbeat their sentiment was showing). So, I picked up the phone and gave them a call. I was surprised when they said they hadn't been receiving any communications from our team. A bit of a nice chat followed by a gentle request for investigation from their end revealed that their "very advanced" company email filters were somehow blocking all communications from our company's email domain. My chat with them revealed that they were very happy with what our product did for them. They were the kind of customers that kept quiet, used what they needed and didn't have the time to go exploring the product beyond what was important to them. But the point here is that we would have never found out, had it not been for that one phone call from a very curious person in the customer success department who wanted to know why there was no response to any outreach going their way.

So, my suggestion to all my SaaS-y friends is to never forget the humans at both ends of the automation. When planned and executed well, your digital-led (and human-supported) strategy can not only increase retention, but also lead to increased advocacy and expansion across your account base.

Part III: Grow

Chapter 9
ROCK AND ROLL TO RENEWALS

"Renewals mark the anniversary of your relationship with customers, and the best gift you can give them is a seamless renewal process as an add-on to the continual love you show them with value realization and success outcomes"

So you've invested an incredible amount of time and effort in strategizing how you can be more customer-centric; you've educated your entire workforce to help them understand your customers better, they have had meaningful touchpoints and great conversations with customers, and the customer's sentiment reflects that they see value in your product. Now it is time to reap the fruits of your labour - it's renewal time! Naturally, with all the memorable moments, wins and value they've received, most of your customers will be ready to renew. Renewals, in most cases, are not a guarantee, but a highly likely outcome of a great customer success strategy.

While showcasing value, outcomes and partnership make the journey to the renewal a fun, engaging and exciting one for the customer (hence the rock and roll reference!), it is crucial to remember that the process of a renewal is still a separate motion and needs to be looked at in that way. The terms renewal and retention are often used interchangeably but they are different from one another. A renewal is so much more than a date on a piece of paper or in your system that defines when a customer's subscription is due for expiry; it is an administrative process which forms a key part of your retention strategy.

Companies follow varied business models in their subscription offerings:

- Offering periodic plans such as monthly, quarterly or annually with the option for customers to automatically renew via a saved payment method on file, or the option to cancel their subscription online before it is renewed (Examples are your Netflix or LinkedIn subscription). With this model, the customer has the option to churn at any point.

- A renewal contract with a set term (mostly annual or multi-year) which has an expiry date, set payment terms and needs to be reviewed and renewed at the end of that period. In this type of model, the involvement of different teams such as legal and procurement on both ends, the contract paperwork, financial negotiations etc., often make for a stressful process and unforeseen delays even when the outcome is meant to be positive.

Some businesses embrace a combination of the above two models to cater to different tiers of customers.

Irrespective of what the renewal model looks like, your customers' journey to value plays a major role in their decision to renew. But the importance of a set renewal process cannot be denied, especially in models where contract signing and reviews are involved. The aim should be to make the renewal as seamless as the rest of your customer journey. So how do you make this process smooth for the champions,users and executive buyers of your product, especially when they don't have much of a role to play in the administrative process apart from agreeing to renew?

Having a renewal strategy that guides your internal team and customers is key to supporting this phase of the customer lifecycle. And that doesn't involve just sending a contract and an invoice a few days before the renewal, it is planning and aligning with any processes at the customer's end with yours. A lot of the things that go into making the sales cycle for new business at your company can be replicated into your renewal strategy to make way for a frictionless process and cut down on approval and wait times.

In this chapter, we explore best practices to ensure a seamless renewal process.

Who Owns Renewals?

The internal ownership for initiating and managing the renewal process varies from company to company. In some businesses, the end to end customer management process is owned by the Customer Success Manager, while others have an account management function dedicated towards the management of upsells, cross-sells and renewals. The rules of engagement for sales, customer success and account management teams depend on your business model and the nature of your contracts with customers.

Just like all other business processes, there is no one-strategy-suits-all approach to renewal ownership, and hence no right or wrong answers to which group within your organization has accountability for renewals. Let's explore the different models for renewal ownership:

1. **Renewals are owned by the CSM**: With an aim to give customers a single point of contact who is their trusted advisor and helps them drive outcomes, some companies use their customer success team to drive the renewal process.

2. **Renewals are owned by the sales team**: In order to keep the customer success team focused on

delivering value, this model passes the renewal conversation into the hands of the sales team.

3. **There is a dedicated renewals manager or account managers:** Most software companies, ranging from startups to enterprises, are now leaning towards a model where dedicated account managers handle commercial discussion and process associated with account expansions (Upsells and cross-sells) and renewals.

Some companies take the hybrid road and use a combination of the above models while handling renewals and expansions. For example, renewals in the smaller or mid-tier accounts that are simply transactable and only involve a straight-forward contract signing and invoicing process are handled by CSMs, while bigger renewals for organizations such as governments or large enterprises where the administrative process involves complicated contracts, negotiations and the involvement of different departments at both ends are best handled by account managers or renewal managers that specialize in this part of the process. For complex customer organization structures, businesses decide to compensate pre-sales teams for expansions in a separate unit of the customer's business. Most companies outline this in their "Rules of Engagement" for pre-sales, account management and customer success teams to clearly define accountabilities, and ensure seamless renewal and expansion operations.

Irrespective of where the accountability of renewals lies, teams should work together to put up a united front while helping the customer through this phase of their lifecycle. Especially in models where a different team comes in to handle the renewal, it is important that they have all the necessary information about the customer's health, sentiment and key contacts from the customer success team before approaching the customer for a renewal. Understanding the roles of different stakeholders at the customer's end and aligning with them using clear communication is crucial. This will require the renewals and customer success teams to be on the same page, and also helps set clear expectations with customers by letting them know what to expect from each team.

Building a Renewal Playbook for High-Value Renewals

Renewal playbooks help your internal teams follow a step by step process for customer renewals and give them guidelines for different scenarios they might come across in the process. Scalable, adaptable and flexible playbooks are a recipe for success as they ensure consistency in the process for your teams and for customers. By helping your team follow a set process, it also allows you to assess what's working well and which part of the renewal cycle needs attention and improvement.

Every organization's renewal playbook is different from another's, and depends on the type of subscription model you follow for your customers, the accountability for renewals and how much work it actually takes to process the renewal contract. There are other factors such as customer health, account risk etc., that also influence the design of your renewal playbook.

So, while there's no single playbook that works for everyone, there are some things that need to be taken into consideration while creating an organizational playbook for renewals:

1. **The pre-work**: The prep work that goes into renewing a customer starts the day they sign up with you and goes into building continual value and helping them achieve their outcomes. But aside from that, there is preparation involved in working towards readiness for the renewal, especially for your high-value accounts. This should start with an internal review of the account between the different teams involved, and a plan to develop the renewal messaging for the customer.

During your internal review, assess different aspects of the customer's health and sentiment. This includes adoption, the strength of your relationship with them, the quality of service provided (using support tickets, responses to feedback, and other digital and human interactions), their financial history with your business (upgrades or downgrades, invoicing history), and any other external factors (such as the state of the customer's business). How you initiate your renewal messaging to the customer depends on the health of the account, how much value was delivered and any risks that the customer success team preempts that might affect the renewal.

My top tip to aid your planning process is to directly ask the "willingness to renew" question as part of the business objectives review session, also commonly known as EBRs or QBRs. Business objective reviews are designed to understand and showcase the value delivered thus far and to listen to customers and their priorities, and are mostly conducted on a quarterly basis. If you're not conducting a business objectives review session with your key customers, go back to Chapter 7 on why you should start doing these. Asking the question about renewal sentiment as part of one of these meetings (preferably the one conducted closest to contract renewal date), opens up an honest conversation about where the customer's "real" sentiment lies and also helps highlight any real red flags that can be addressed before the risk goes up any higher.

All of this feeds into your internal planning and strategy to approach the renewal.

2. **The Renewal Notice**: Timing is of the essence in the initiation of renewal conversations. Closer to the time of the renewal (ideally 90 days ahead), formal communication needs to be sent to the customer to highlight that the contract is close to expiring and that you wish to kick off the renewal process. Make sure you clearly outline the next steps (such as dates, length of contract, proces from your end), and send this to the right stakeholders who approve the renewal and facilitate the start of the renewal process from the customer's side.

This is usually followed by a conversation to discuss any additional licensing needs, contract consolidation and even consider the possibility of an early renewal. One thing that good account managers or anyone else who is responsible for renewals would do is align with the customer's budget approval cycle. Most big companies follow their financial year or calendar year cycle to get pre-approved budgeting for the systems they want to use in the following year. Staying closely aligned with your decision makers on the customer's side helps you get some insights on that approval and helps you with accurately forecasting any risks to renewal. It is also a good chance to present the benefits of an early renewal with customers who have seen faster time to value with your product and help them take advantage of any early renewal incentives you have in place. Any reluctance from a customer who in your eyes is healthy sentiment-wise should be seen as a red flag and monitored closely for coexistence or penetration of competitive products and also to assess if they really have received enough value from your product with respect to their goals.

3. **Cross-Departmental Collaboration**: This is true for both parties, the customer and the seller.

   On your side, make sure you start the process early by getting paperwork ready in advance, and understanding the key stakeholders and personnel involved from the customer's side. Make the contract, invoicing and payments process as seamless as you can for your customers.

Since you don't have much control over the customer's approval and procurement processes, you can only influence the process from the outside using your champions and executive decision makers to push things forward at their end. Anyone who handles high value renewals with enterprise customers has to be equipped with the skills to deal with procurement departments, negotiations and a bit of legalese to help the customer navigate the nuances of the contract with ease if needed. It is one of the reasons I am a supporter of the "tag-team" model for high-value renewals, where customer success and account management/sales teams work in close collaboration and bring together the best of both worlds to make the renewal process and contract signing seamless for the customer. The customer success department handles the piece where we quantify the value delivered and make the case for the renewal to happen while sales/ account management teams go ahead and take on the negotiations, contracting and invoicing bits.

A well-led renewal conversation is the perfect example of "Team work makes the dream work"

4. **Managing Risk and Delays**: Life isn't perfect, and the same is true for renewal situations.

Even when the outcome is eventually positive, there could be risks and delays associated with the processing of some customer's renewals due to several unforeseen reasons. Budget cuts, unprecedented times and evolving business needs may need you to make room for risk management and negotiations.

Aside from the obvious skills of patience and empathy that are key in all customer situations, remember that leading negotiations with the "benefit you are providing to the customer" will give you an upper hand. There are often situations where your customer champions are advocating internally but are receiving push back from their procurement or executive teams and are forced to re-negotiate. Be prepared to help your champions by facilitating this discussion and offering to be a part of it if it helps make the chain of conversations shorter.

Even if you have a customer with an unhealthy sentiment index, my suggestion is to avoid going for a short-sighted strategy that saves the renewal in the current cycle, but leaves the customer at a risk of mid-term churn in the future. Put the focus on why the relationship is at risk and determine your next steps from there. If there is a gap in understanding in the customer's definition of success and yours, then monetary discounts alone will not fix that gap, but a continual effort into helping the customer will. On the other hand, if the customer is genuinely facing budget issues and business challenges, good-faith discounts go a long way in strengthening the relationship. The most important aspect of this is understanding the reason behind the risk and offering a solution that aligns with your common goals.

Scaling Your Renewal Process

Digitization is your saviour when it comes to replicating the efficiency of your high-value renewals program across the rest of your customer base, with a few careful considerations. The same health and sentiment metrics that feed into your high value renewal strategy work for your other renewals too. What changes is the length and complexity of the procurement process associated with enterprise renewals. And that allows you the chance to execute renewals digitally with a touch of human intervention as and when it is needed by your customers.

As with a high-touch renewal program, the importance of clear, concise and personalized communication is important for your scaled renewal process too. This could be via an in-product notification and /or an email reminding them of the upcoming renewal and what to expect in the period post the renewal such as upcoming features, exciting value-adds, benefits for long-time customers, and anything else that highlights and adds value to your relationship.

Renewal Surveys

Renewal surveys are hugely effective in helping gauge the renewal sentiment and understanding next steps. This could be a simple one-question survey asking about their "willingness to renew" and can be supplemented with a report of usage or any other metrics that showcase the value and importance of your product in the customer's world. Based on the response to that survey, you can either follow up with a renewal contract and/or invoice and the next steps in the process, or with a request for a follow up conversation in case of a negative response. In either scenario, it is important to lead with value and understand the reasoning behind the customer's decision and to offer help if they need it.

There could be a third scenario where there is no response to your renewal survey. This could be due to several reasons such as change of ownership, change of mind, lack of championship, or an honest miss when your email lands in spam or goes unread. Flag these customers for manual follow up and ensure they're aware that their contract is due for expiry.

Automatic Renewals

Giving your customers the option to set their contracts up in a way that allows for automatic renewal at the end of their term is a great way to minimize the transactional process in every renewal cycle. However, it is crucial to give customers advance notice of the upcoming renewal even when they've set their subscription to auto-renew. Make it easy for them to cancel automatic renewals if they need to, update their registered payment method, and have a clear cancellation policy in place to avoid customer dissatisfaction and refund hassles.

Also ensure that you make your customers aware of all the options for completing their renewal such as automatic renewal, manual contract signing or a self-serviced, digitally led process. Sometimes, company policies evolve and prevent customers from setting up automatic payments with vendors, and letting your customers know they have other options if this happens goes a long way in helping make their lives easy and saving time in choosing the method that works best for them.

Don't Forget to Say Thank You!

A quick "thank you" email or note to the customer can go a long way in letting the customer know that they've not been forgotten after the renewal transaction and reinforces that they made a good decision by choosing to continue their partnership with you. This is especially crucial in the scaled renewal motion to convey the emotion and importance of your partnership, because with high-value renewals, this conversation mostly happens naturally when you converse with the customer.

Continuing on The Journey of Success After The Renewal

Once the renewal has been completed successfully, continue on the journey of showing value to your customers by capturing their goals and priorities for the coming term and maintain the continuity of conversations which assure the customer that you are interested in their long term success.

Another aspect of this success journey after the renewal is how it feeds into continually improving your internal processes and ensuring the accuracy of your renewal forecasts. So, make sure to capture any learnings, things that work and things that don't so that your renewal process can evolve with the evolving nature of your customers' businesses.

Non-Renewals: Difficult Conversations About Undesirable Outcomes

No matter how well you do in maintaining continual value-based relationships, sometimes churn is inevitable. Customers leave, and while it is not the desired outcome for any company, it is a situation that businesses need to be prepared for. So, when you know it's time to let go and no amount of effort will be enough to convince the customer to stay with you, make sure you plan a graceful exit that keeps the integrity of your relationship intact.

Offboarding

Your customer's off-boarding journey is as important as their onboarding journey, albeit not as exciting for you. If your customers have important data or information stored within your platform or product which they need help in extracting as part of their exit process, be sure to offer them some guidance, time and help if they need it. Depending on your contract and exit negotiations, this can be offered as a free or paid service.

The effort you put into making the offboarding experience a good one goes a long way in helping the customer remember how easy you are to do business with. Also, don't forget to tell them they are welcome to come back in the future.

Exit Interviews

Customer exit interviews and surveys are another huge part of that graceful exit strategy, not to mention a goldmine of learning for you. These are often ignored by companies or not done at all because who wants to talk to a customer that's definitely leaving (and that's the mindset that needs to change). The information from such an initiative feeds into your product and go-to-market strategy, your support and success programs, and how you fare against competitors in the market. Also, if the customer is really leaving for reasons that have nothing to do with your business but more to do with theirs, knowing that helps you assess if there is a chance of them coming back in the future. Since these surveys and interviews are designed for customers who are leaving, they are also harder to get responses to, so focus on direct, simple questions and don't forget to be empathetic to their cause of leaving, no matter what it is.

In the end, your relationship with a customer is much bigger than a lost renewal. Contracts end, but relationships can still be maintained. Your champions and the trust you build with them goes wherever they go. It is crucial to understand the long term benefits of relationship building against the short-term loss of not being able to secure the renewal. It all boils down to the human connection and how you convey ingenuity towards your customers in not only understanding what draws them towards your business but also showing an equal amount of interest in what caused them to pull away.

Chapter 10
CUSTOMER SUCCESS AS A GROWTH ENGINE

So you've finally made it to the last chapter. Congratulations on unlocking your first steps towards building a customer success mindset. One thing to remember is that even though the fundamentals remain the same, your journey towards customer-centricity could look very different from that of other companies, even those offering products and services very similar to yours. This pathway that stems from keeping your customers at the centre of your operations inspires great business results and positively influences your retention, expansion and acquisition strategy.

Now that we've talked about the why and the how of a customer success mindset in parts 1 and 2 of the book, let's explore the growth opportunities that come from being customer-centric, how you can continue your customer-centricity journey by empowering your C-Suite with the skills and thinking of a Chief Customer Officer and the power of a great customer advocacy program.

From Add-on to Imperative: The Future of Customer Success

Just like your journey in reading this book and discovering customer-centric thought processes that you either didn't know about, or knew but never thought of applying to your professional role, the very concept of customer success has also taken a journey to be at the stage of maturity that it is today. Even though customer success, since its inception, was always designed to be a growth engine, like any transformational idea that changes the way we do things, it has gone through a maturity curve.

Years ago, companies started adding a customer success department to their organizational structure to show customers they were following the latest trends in software and were customer focused. But the role definition and operations of the customer success team were far away from the principles of customer-centricity and customer success often ended up being the "everything" department with miscellaneous responsibilities from a mix of sales to customer support and service. As companies started to recognize and understand the power of implementing an effective strategy for customer-centricity, they started to put effort and investment in hiring leaders and teams whose roles were aligned with the concept of customer success. Now with most organizations finally getting the grasp of the "why" of customer success (better late than never), the next mountain to be moved in the maturity model for customer-centricity is at what point in their growth curve does a company start to think about customer success?

Change in an organization's strategy for growth and development is either influenced by external factors such as market need, or internal factors such as change in structure, cost-saving or mergers and acquisition. One of the other reasons that drives strategic change in organizations is the hard way, through failure, chaos and dissatisfaction of employees and customers.

Startups are usually focused on closing net new sales as their key strategy for increased profitability, and only start to think about renewals and customer success when they start to see a significant amount of churn in their acquired customer base. Historically and even currently, a majority of businesses start their journey towards customer success quite late due to the lack of a budget for dedicated customer success team or business structure.

While each company may decide to start a dedicated function to focus on customer success at a different point in their business journey, it is imperative to start thinking about what matters to your customers and what makes them stay early on. Adopting a customer-centric thinking in your business model helps you drive your growth objectives and in identifying the key drivers that enhance retention as well as acquisition of new customers. It also helps to build a strategy around services that can offer further opportunities for growth of revenue. An early focus on customer-centricity also helps your employees adapt to that culture from the get-go, and before you know it, it becomes ingrained in your way of being as you scale your operations.

What I described above is not only best practice for early stage startups, it is also my prediction for the future of customer success. Given the risks of not being customer-centric are quite scary (no one in the world runs a business without aiming for it to be successful), companies with a futuristic thinking will build their customer-centricity and success practice and adopt the customer success mindset from the outset to listen to their customers' needs and deliver products and services that help them stay relevant in the long run.

If you don't have the budget for a team, start simple with building resources that aid customer onboarding, such as help content that customers can access within your application or on your website. You can also start mapping your customer journey and talking to your early customers to understand their definition and metrics associated with success, and getting feedback in the form of NPS, CSAT, interviews etc (we talked about these metrics in detail in Chapter 6). Mapping this journey will guide your teams in the right direction on where the customer experience can be improved, and will build the foundation for a company-wide customer success mindset. As you scale up and bring on a team and a leader dedicated towards customer success, those initial foundations will help you scale and mature your retention and growth strategy very quickly rather than undergoing a change management process (which most organizations currently do), to re-establish the foundations of customer-centricity. That is a lot of time, money and effort saved just by starting early; plus the efficiency that comes from understanding your customer's lifecycle and ways to improve how flow from one stage to another is invaluable.

With competition increasing and people's attention spans being very limited, no business can afford to be just another brand that offers a product or service that people use but never remember. The way you instil your brand value into your customer's hearts and minds makes all the difference, and instilling the customer success mindset into your operational values is imperative to your brand reputation and growth.

The benefits of being focused on your customer's success are so vast and varied that even though this strategy was originally developed for and majorly adopted by SaaS technology businesses, companies in the non-SaaS world are quickly hopping on to the growth bandwagon by employing customer success and centricity as a key part of their strategy. Famous brands like restaurant chain KFC and American domestic merchandise retailer Bed Bath and Beyond are prime examples of non-SaaS brands that have recently appointed their first Chief Customer Officers with a view to bring the needs of the customer to the board room and invest in their financial growth through customer loyalty.

Chief Customer Officer: The Role that Brings the Customer into the Boardroom

I mentioned in the initial parts of the book that customer success and customer-centricity are not functional initiatives, they require a constant and conscious effort that starts with leadership buy-in. The role of a Chief Customer Officer (CCO) is imperative to ensure the voice of the customer is heard in the boardroom and is converted into actions that encourage customer-centricity. This powerful role in the C-Suite is tasked with driving profitability by leveraging the power of a customer-centric practice that drives the business towards customer-led growth. Executive-level accountability for customer value helps the business in gaining an accurate understanding of the strategic drivers specific to your product or service that contribute to customers' buying and retention decisions. A CCO not only brings thought leadership from a customer success point of view, but also a strong commercial acumen that helps them quantify customer value and business expansion. In most businesses, the teams that service and grow the customer after their acquisition sit under the CCO. These are:

- Renewals and Expansion (Account Management)
- Customer onboarding, deployment and customer success
- Professional Services
- Customer Support
- Customer Marketing and Advocacy
- Partner and Reseller Success (Channel Success)

With these key teams under their wing and a strong understanding of how to tie the sales and marketing strategy with customer outcomes, the CCO role helps drive efficiency, scalability and adaptability in the customer and company's growth journey. And giving the representative of the customer's needs a seat at the table ensures the entire leadership team stays committed to a customer-centric approach and are able to understand the profitability associated with this strategy when they see numbers that quantify the benefits and customer loyalty that adds the qualitative aspect to really drive the point home about why customer-centricity is everything.

I talked to Maranda Dziekonski, CCO at Swiftly. Maranda is an inspirational leader and a well-renowned name in the global customer success community. She says, *"Everyone in the organization owns the success of the customer. Everyone! And while this is not new, what is new is how organizations are realizing the power of a strong customer success motion. Customer Success is a growth multiplier, and unlocking that power within your organization can be a game-changer. This is where the Chief Customer Officer role comes in.*

The role of the CCO has evolved from an individual that sat siloed in the Customer Success function, helped mitigate churn, and made sure everything post-sale was taken care of, to the strategic layer that partners with everyone in the entire organization to ensure that the goals of the customers are top of mind while balancing out the business needs. This is a delicate ecosystem, and a strong CCO can help drive both the strategy and tactics required to do this."

This incredible understanding of how organizational culture and profitability is tied to customers, and a unique skill set that combines understanding of customer value with sales, marketing and professional service design is setting CCO's up to take on other executive roles as part of their career journey. Airline giant Qantas and one of Australia's largest private health insurance providers Medibank have recently named their CCO's as their next

CEOs. This speaks strongly to the power of a customer-centric strategy and how organizations are working to put the customer at the centre of their operations.

Shifting the Goal Post: Fuel your Growth through Customer Advocacy

The biggest direct advantage that you can see from having a customer success mindset and investing in efforts and resources for customer-centricity is earning the loyalty and trust of the majority of your customers. But with people getting busier by the minute, you need to put some effort into ensuring that you have a way of helping your brand advocates with ways to share their message about your business. That's where a well-planned customer advocacy program comes into play. The joint accountability for your customer advocacy program lies with your customer success and marketing department, or your customer marketing department (if your business has the budget and resources to build this separate arm). With the right strategic approach, you can successfully translate your customers' love for your business into an opportunity for marketing and growth.

Building and growing your base of customer advocates comes from the continual effort you put in making customers successful and improving your customer-centricity strategy. But how do you identify advocates from your customer base? A good way to start is to identify the characteristics of a customer who would fit your "Ideal advocate profile". You can use this profile as a benchmark while contacting customers and inviting them to be part of your advocacy program. Customers with a promoter NPS sentiment, or customers that are able to see early time to value in their journey with you based on the metrics you capture as part of your data strategy are great candidates for inviting into your advocacy program. Talk to your account management and customer success teams so that they can validate the story behind the metrics and data and if it is a good time to reach out to the customer for advocacy efforts.

The aim of your advocacy program is to enable your customer advocates to engage with your business and show their love through different channels that help increase your brand's awareness and growth. This can be done in numerous ways:

- **Testimonials and Case Studies**: Sharing testimonials in a video or a written quote about how your product has improved a customer's way of working. A number of public review sites such as TrustRadius, Gartner Peer Reviews and G2 allow people to leave reviews about your business and are used as trusted sources of information by potential customers of your brand. Inviting your customer advocates to leave their positive opinion of your brand on these sites is a powerful way of showcasing your focus on customer-centricity for increased brand awareness.

You can also do case studies in the form of videos, or a white paper that sits on your website for people to watch or read. Good case studies tie the customer's problem statement to your brand's vision and mission and help paint a picture of the transformational experience you provide to your customers not only through your product but also through the positive experiences in their journey with you.

- **Collaboration in Webinars/Podcasts/ Conferences**: Asking your customer advocates to speak with you at public events conducted by you or at industry events is a great way to showcase the collaboration between your businesses and the mutual benefits you have received through your partnership.

- **References for Prospective Customers**: Again, people love networking and interacting with people who do similar things as they do. Keeping a few customers on your list who have agreed to act as references for potential deals you are about to close is a great way to foster the foundations of trust with potential customers and also to showcase to your existing customers who agree to act as references how much you trust them with such a conversation.

- **Experts on your Customer Community**: Inviting your customer champions and advocates to contribute to your customer community by interacting with other customers and answering their questions enables two-way communication and networking through your product, and that goes a long way in helping your advocates build and grow their network, all while promoting your brand by converting more of your users into champions like themselves.

Measuring Growth Driven By Customer Advocacy: Existing Customer Referrals are Real

Turning your existing customers into advocates can bring a huge amount of new business growth through referrals. In fact, businesses are now increasingly making use of a metric called **Earned Growth Rate (EGR) to track their revenue growth through referrals from existing customers.** Earned growth calculates your revenue growth from returning customers and any new business via referrals. It takes into account:

- **Net Revenue Retention (NRR)**, the percentage rate of your total recurring revenue including expansions, downsells and churn against your total recurring revenue from existing customers during a given time. We've talked about this metric in Chapter 5.

- **Earned New Customers (ENC),** which can be simply defined as the percentage of revenue from customers who have been referred to your business by your existing customers versus the total revenue from all new customers.

  Earned growth rate is the sum of your NRR and ENC percentages subtracted by 100.

Dickey Singh at cast.app truly believes that EGR is the new NPS. He says *"It is essential to think how effectively referrals translate into revenue for your business and EGR is the perfect metric for that"*.

My biggest tip for your customer success program is to shift the goal post for your team from renewal to advocacy. If your team strives to serve each customer not like they were at risk of losing them, but with a view to make them so happy that they become raving fans, you will experience the magic of true customer delight for your business and the growth that comes along with it.

Final Thoughts

Whether it's walking into a bookstore and being handed a title that you would love to read, or getting a hot pizza at the right moment when you're hungry, or travelling to a city you've always wanted to go to and having the time of your life; humans are driven by emotions that come from memorable moments.

How you impact your customers' emotions is as important as impacting their bottomline using the products and services you sell. Customer-centricity is a journey not a destination, and it matures with the growth of your organization. The important thing is to never let go of the *customer success mindset.*